INSIDE
THE
RED
TENT

Popular Insights

Solving the DaVinci Code Mystery
Brandon Gilvin

Wisdom from the Five People You Meet in Heaven
Brandon Gilvin and Heather Godsey

Unveiling the Secret Life of Bees
Amy Lignitz Harken

Gifts of Gilead
Amy Lignitz Harken
Lee Hull Moses

In Search of the Kite Runner
Judi Slayden Hayes

Inside the Red Tent
Sandra Hack Polaski

INSIDE
THE
RED
TENT

SANDRA HACK POLASKI

CHALICE®
PRESS

ST. LOUIS, MISSOURI

Cover image: Cynthia Huff
Cover and interior design: Elizabeth Wright

ChalicePress.com

ISBN 978-0-827230-28-6

Printed in the United States of America

Contents

Acknowledgments

As in raising a child, it takes a village to write a book. In particular, thanks are due:

To Trent Butler and the staff at Chalice Press, who had confidence that I could write this book.

To Sandie Gravett, who helped me see that I could write it, and Karla Bohmbach, who steered me in right directions.

To Jeanette Holt, Anne Shelley, Suzanne Stovall Vinson, and others whose enthusiasm for the novel helped me understand why this book needed to be written.

To Nancy Waldo and Denise Bennett, who pointed me toward storytelling resources.

To Juliana Claassens, who read the manuscript and offered valuable suggestions.

To Don Polaski, who read drafts, suggested improvements, and listened.

To Hannah and Will Polaski, who put up with Mommy's preoccupation with writing, and who reminded me that there was a world outside my work.

To all the communities of women who are sustained by the power of story.

Introducing the Characters
of *The Red Tent*

Asher—son of Jacob and Zilpah.

Benia—husband of Dinah late in her life. Dinah meets this carpenter and widower in Egypt after her son is nearly grown. Benia marries Dinah, and they spend the rest of their lives together.

Benjamin—youngest son of Jacob and Rachel.

Bilhah—handmaid to Rachel, daughter of Laban by a slave, had son Dan by Jacob.

Dan—son of Jacob and Bilhah.

Deborah—female acolytes to Rebecca, who calls *all* her acolytes "Deborah."

Dinah—daughter of Jacob and Leah, Jacob's eleventh child and only daughter. Mother of Re-mose by Shalem and wife of Benia late in life.

Esau—twin brother of Jacob, father of Tabea.

Gad—son of Jacob and Zilpah.

Gera—daughter of Dinah's brother Benjamin. When Dinah returns to Canaan with Joseph, Gera tells Dinah about the rest of her brothers' offspring and recites various family stories, including the story of Dinah herself.

Hamor—ruler of the city of Shechem, husband of Re-nefer, father of Shalem.

Hori—son of Meryt.

Inna—midwife who tends Jacob's wives in childbirth and teaches Rachel her midwife skills.

Isaac—father of Jacob and Esau.

Issachar—son of Jacob and Leah.

Jacob—son of Isaac and Rebecca, grandson of Abraham and Sarah. Unlike his father-in-law, Laban, Jacob acknowledges all his children by Leah, Rachel, Bilhah, and Zilpah, even though Bilhah and Zilpah are slaves.

Joseph—first son of Jacob and Rachel, acquires the name Zafenat Paneh-ah in Egypt.

Judah—son of Jacob and Leah.

Kiya—one of Menna and Shif-re's children, becomes especially close to Dinah.

✗ **Laban**— father of all four of Jacob's wives, each by a different woman.

Leah—Dinah's mother, first to marry Jacob, recognized as a daughter of Laban because of her freeborn mother. Leah's sons are Reuben, Simon, Levi, Judah, Zebulun, Naphtali, and Issachar.

Levi—son of Jacob and Leah.

Menna—son of Meryt. After the deaths of Re-nefer and Nakht-re, Dinah and Meryt live with Menna and his wife, Shif-re.

Meryt—midwife who delivers Dinah's son. Like Inna and Rachel before them, Meryt and Dinah become colleagues and friends.

Nakht-re—brother of Re-nefer. Re-nefer and Dinah live with his family when they return to Egypt.

Naphtali—son of Jacob and Leah.

Rachel—wife of Jacob, Joseph's mother, recognized as a daughter of Laban because of her freeborn mother. Her two sons, Joseph and Benjamin, are younger than any of her sisters' children because she was barren for many years.

Rebecca—wife of Isaac, Esau and Jacob's mother. Later in her life, she becomes an oracle who lives at the sacred grove of Mamre.

✔ **Re-mose**—son of Shalem and Dinah, whom Dinah bears in Egypt after Shalem's death. He is named Re-mose by his grandmother, who is the child's legal guardian. Dinah wishes to call him Bar-Shalem, which means "son of Shalem," but Re-nefer forbids her to do so.

Re-nefer—wife of Hamor, mother of Shalem.

Reuben—oldest son of Jacob, first son of Jacob and Leah.

Ruti—wife of Laban late in his life. She has two sons by Laban, and both he and the sons treat her badly.

* **Shalem**—Dinah's lover, oldest child of Hamor and Re-nefer, father of Re-mose. (In the biblical text, his name is Shechem, the same as the name of the city; *The Red Tent* author Diamant gives him a separate, personal name.)

Shery—Zafenat Paneh-ah's servant, tells Dinah the story of her master's (Joseph's) rise to power.

Simon—son of Jacob and Leah (Simeon in the biblical text).

Tabea—cousin of Dinah, daughter of Esau who is close to Dinah's age.

Werenro—Rebecca's messenger, whom Dinah meets initially at Mamre and later in Egypt.

Zafenat Paneh-ah—the name acquired by Jacob and Rachel's son Joseph after he becomes the Egyptian king's vizier. Re-mose is assigned to be his scribe.

Zebulun—son of Jacob and Leah.

Zilpah—handmaid to Leah, daughter of Laban by a slave, had sons Gad and Asher by Jacob.

Introduction

The Red Tent presents us a tale of rebirth reminiscent of an ancient saga: an author imagines a story, develops it into a book, sees it through to publication—and then watches helplessly while it languishes on store shelves. The book is eventually allowed to go out of print, but still the author does not give up. She buys up the remaindered copies, gathers a list of addresses of Reform Jewish rabbis, and begins mailing the book around the country in a determined attempt to find a readership. Her effort is finally rewarded. The book catches on and becomes a best-seller.

Readers who now encounter *The Red Tent* may find it difficult to fathom how this powerful, intimate story failed to catch on in its first publication. The book expands on a story generally familiar to Jewish and Christian readers, the story of Jacob, grandson of Abraham and son of Isaac, and his wives Leah and Rachel. Jacob, however, is not the main character in this retelling. He is more the occasion for the narrative than a significant character in it.

Unlike the biblical version, *The Red Tent* is female-centered rather than male-centered. Yet neither Leah nor Rachel is its main character, though they are two of the narrative's most

1

vital forces. Instead the story follows, and is told from the point of view of, Dinah, the only daughter of Jacob named in the biblical narrative, and the subject of a strange, violent episode sandwiched in the biblical text between Jacob's reunion with his brother Esau and the stories of Joseph.

This passage, the 34th chapter of Genesis, has long troubled biblical scholars and nonacademic readers alike. It is full of violence and deceit, with questionable motives on all sides. It expresses extreme xenophobia, an attitude reflected elsewhere in the Hebrew Bible but by no means the Hebrew Bible's only perspective on foreigners. And, as women readers in particular have noted, it is a story about a woman that is not, ultimately, about the woman. Dinah never speaks, acts only once, and is absent from the narrated action for most of the story. Those who might claim to be acting in her best interests seem to have other motives in mind. At the end of the chapter, Dinah vanishes mysteriously from the biblical narrative, with no word as to her fate.

Author Anita Diamant has chosen this daunting story as her launching point, and this Dinah, so long silenced, speaks through the novel's pages. But Diamant's book is not a horror story. The deceit and violence of Genesis 34 are present, with wrenching consequences. Yet on balance *The Red Tent* is more uplifting and hopeful than it is shocking and painful, and not only because Dinah reveals that her sexual encounter was a consensual relationship, not a rape.

The Red Tent is hopeful and uplifting because it offers an alternative view of what many Bible readers have often imagined was the lonely and miserable life of early biblical women. In place of isolated drudgery or bitter wrangling it depicts women who share their lives together, fully experiencing joy and sorrow. They love one another deeply, even when their shared circumstances mean that they cause one another pain. They pass on their knowledge, their rituals, and their stories to the next generation, and with these their identity and their strength. Even when events result in the most tragic consequences, these women survive, discover new support networks, and live on to see another joyful day.

The compelling nature of this community of women is the main reason *The Red Tent* has found such an enthusiastic following. But the novel also raises a number of questions, which this companion volume seeks to address. We have already mentioned that Dinah appears as a character in the Hebrew Bible in a single episode, in Genesis 34, and that this text is a strange and difficult one. Chapter 1 of this book explores the biblical text in greater detail, demonstrating why so many different conclusions have been read out of the same text. By exploring this story closely, we will be better able to appreciate Diamant's choices in reading Dinah's story as she does, while understanding how others, even other feminist readers, have seen something very different in these verses.

The Red Tent is not only a reading of a biblical text; it is also a reconstruction of a certain period in ancient history. In chapter 2, we will look at the historical evidence of this period, particularly for women. We will see why the historical record is not easy to reconstruct and why a certain amount of imagination is also required to bring ordinary women of the ancient world to life. We will also explore, in some detail, what is known about ancient childbirth practices, since these practices play such an important role in the life of Diamant's Dinah.

As a reflection on and retelling of a Hebrew Bible text, *The Red Tent* stands in a long line of Jewish interpretation known collectively as *midrash*. Because Christian readers, in particular, may not be familiar with the tradition of midrash, Chapter 3 discusses what midrash is and briefly explores retellings of the stories of Leah, Rachel, and Dinah from the early centuries C.E. to contemporary midrashists. These stories, we will find, have long held fascination for readers of the Hebrew Bible, and various meanings have been read out of the texts.

Chapter 4 addresses questions about God. *The Red Tent* takes us back to a time before monotheism, when even the ancestors of the Israelites worshiped gods and goddesses in great variety. We will sort out some of their stories and gain greater understanding of how religious rituals functioned in ordinary people's lives.

One of the most important aspects of Dinah's story is her relationships—with her mother, aunts, and brothers in Mesopotamia and Canaan; with her loves in Canaan and Egypt; and with the new families of which she becomes a part after she is wrenchingly separated from the family that gave her birth. In chapter 5 we will consider each of these relationships, and how they contribute to the person that Dinah becomes in the novel's pages.

In *The Red Tent*, Dinah tells her own story in her own voice. This first-person narrative is a great deal of what makes this story so compelling and causes it to ring so true with readers who share little or none of the narrator's historical or social context. In the final chapter, we will consider the importance of telling stories, particularly personal stories, with Dinah as our guide.

Diamant's novel is at once intensely personal and deeply relational. You may choose to read it on your own or in a study or discussion group. If you are reading *The Red Tent* alone, you are likely to identify strongly with the first-person narrator, through whose perspective the whole story is told. If you are a woman reading this book with other women, your experience of the book may spur you to create or rediscover rituals that celebrate your life together as women.

Either way, this study guide is designed to help you think through some of the questions that may arise as you read and to enhance your reading of the novel. May you experience, in your reading and reflection, the blessing that Diamant's Dinah bestows on those who come to hear her story.

CHAPTER 1

What Happened to Dinah?

> *Near the beginning of your holy book, there is a passage
> that seems to say I was raped and continues with the bloody
> tale of how my honor was avenged.*
>
> (*Red Tent*, 1)
>
> *Now Dinah the daughter of Leah, whom she had borne to
> Jacob, went out to visit the women of the region.*
>
> (Gen. 34:1)

The biblical story of Dinah is not clear regarding what
happened to her. For readers of the English Bible, this is likely
to be a surprising assertion. After all, many English Bibles
head this section of Genesis "The Rape of Dinah." The Hebrew verb describing what Shechem did to Dinah is variously
translated "defiled" her, "violated" her, "humbled" her, or
"lay with her by force" (Gen. 34:2), and Jacob's sons are angry
because "such a thing ought not to be done" (v. 7).

Yet the more closely we look at this passage, the more
difficult it becomes to discern what the biblical author thinks
about Dinah's own experience. We discover that Dinah's
experience is not the concern of the text. As pointed out by

several commentators, Genesis 34 is not really Dinah's story. She is the occasion for the action, but after the opening lines she becomes an object rather than a subject, a pawn in a social and political story. Her physical absence for most of the story, and the absence of her voice throughout the narrative, are clues to the perceptive reader of the narrator's disinterest in Dinah herself.

For many contemporary readers, though, the question of Dinah's own experience is primary. Was the sexual encounter with Shechem forced or consensual? That is, in modern terms, was it rape?

Strong feminist voices may be heard on both sides of the question. On one side is the characterization given to Diamant's Dinah and followed by several other contemporary commentators. The perspective of the biblical text, they say, is incapable of doing justice to women as persons capable of choice. When a woman does make a choice, particularly if that choice concerns her own body, the text ignores her volition. The violation of Dinah's body, they argue, is entirely in the minds of Jacob's sons (Jacob's own perspective is a matter of debate). Responsible reading, particularly woman-focused reading, does not uncritically adopt the perspective of the male characters in the text, but investigates more carefully to discern the nuances of the story as it is narrated.

From the opposite point of view come the voices of those who champion the perspective of the rape survivor. They point out how often rape is denied or covered up in historical medical and legal literature, and eloquently argue that the right reading is the one that does not silence the victim. Simeon and Levi act to end their sister's exploitation, but their violent response serves to perpetuate the cycle of violence. The rape of one (Dinah) becomes the rape of many (the women of Shechem).

Both these arguments are rooted in the text of Genesis 34. A close look at the biblical narrative will help us see the difficulty of discerning Dinah's own story there.

The Encounter with Shechem

Dinah Goes Out

The Genesis account of Dinah's encounter with Shechem and its aftermath begins, "Now Dinah the daughter of Leah, whom she had borne to Jacob, went out to visit the women of the region" (34:1).

Already the astute reader notices unusual features. Dinah is identified primarily with her mother. She is not "Jacob's daughter by Leah." Her father already seems distant.

We are not told why Dinah "went out," leaving behind the protection of her family's settlement. Diamant offers a scenario that does not require initiative on Dinah's part. She goes to the city with Rachel to attend a birth, and returns there when she is invited by the young mother.

Others have expressed more suspicion regarding Dinah's motives. Noting that Leah "went out" to Jacob to sleep with him (Gen. 30:16), some commentators have claimed that Dinah, like her mother, "went out" looking for sex or at least inviting trouble. By blaming the victim, such readings transfer culpability for the entire sequence of events to the woman.

Setting aside such misogynistic readings, what could have led Dinah to "go out" to people foreign to her? Perhaps Dinah is hoping that she will be chosen and honorably courted as a prospective wife, not smuggled unwanted into the marriage bed, as Leah had been. Or Dinah, lonely and naive, without young female companionship, places too much confidence in the codes of hospitality to which she was accustomed. She may have been initially intrigued by the young foreign man who appears in 34:2, and even accepted an invitation to his home, assuming that the protection of a guest under one's roof was a sacred duty in his family as much as in hers. Or Dinah may be seen as not at all naive, but self-aware and intent on expressing an attitude of openness toward foreigners. However, her open attitude is quelled, ultimately violently, by her brothers' xenophobia.

In any case, Dinah's "going out" signals to the reader of Genesis a new beginning, the start of a new episode in the text. Someone who "goes out" will sooner or later have an encounter, and that encounter will lead to a series of events—for good or for ill.

The Encounter

> And Shechem, son of Hamor the Hivite, prince of the land, saw her, and he seized her and he lay [with] her and he violated her. (Gen. 34:2, au. trans.)

Shechem's position as a "prince of the land" is crucial to the story's progress. Because he is prominent, and his father, Hamor, is a leading man of the city, Shechem and Hamor are able to persuade their fellow citizens to undergo the painful rite of circumcision. Beyond this plot detail, Shechem's social status may be read in one of two ways. Charitably, Shechem's princely status increases Dinah's honor (or at least minimizes her dishonor) in being taken as his wife before proper negotiations are concluded with her family. Uncharitably, Shechem may be seen as a member of the ruling class accustomed to having what he wants on his own terms without concern for the welfare of others. Either way the involvement of a "prince" ratchets up the dramatic tension for readers of the story.

And what does this Shechem, this "prince," do with or to Dinah? Three Hebrew verbs are in focus, each with "her" as its grammatical object. First, Shechem "seized" Dinah. Depending on context, this common word is sometimes translated as mildly as "took" or as forcefully as "grabbed." It is the word the Hebrew Bible often uses for marriage, when a man "takes" a woman into their new home, ending the period of betrothal and beginning their wedded life. But the word clearly can mean an act of force, such as kidnapping or the unlawful seizure of property.

Next, he "lay [with] her." To say that Shechem "laid" Dinah conjures American slang connotations. Still, some commentators find it significant that there is no preposition here. Dinah is the grammatical direct object of the verb denoting Shechem's act, a nuance that some see as indicative of his attitude toward her, treating her as an object rather than a person. Others counter that, while saying that Shechem "lay [with]" Dinah strongly connotes sexual intercourse, the word does not imply force.

The most contested verb of the series is the last, for which we have suggested "he violated her." Sometimes it is read with the verb before as a hendiadys: "he lay with her" + "he violated her" = "he lay with her by force." The word implies debasing, degradation, or shame and is used in contexts in which forcible rape is clearly present, such as Amnon's violation of Tamar in 2 Samuel 13. Yet its primary connotation is humiliation, not force. In Genesis 34 the point of this word's use may be the degradation Dinah experiences by having intercourse before the proper negotiations were made for her marriage. Shechem's offer, it might be inferred, would have been futile if it had been made while Dinah was still a virgin. Now that her status is changed, Shechem and his father have every intention of converting her temporary humiliation into the honorable status of royal wife. Nonetheless, Shechem's social superiority, the nuances of force present in the verbs, and the economy of language with which they are expressed work together in the other direction, to suggest that this is an act of degradation in which Shechem may not have Dinah's best interests at heart.

The Aftermath

The burden of proof is on those who categorize Dinah's experience as rape to explain the next action in the narrative:

> And his soul was drawn to Dinah daughter of Jacob; he loved the girl, and spoke tenderly to her. So Shechem spoke to his father Hamor, saying, "Get me this girl to be my wife." (34:3–4)

Rape, as we understand it today, is an act of domination and profound disrespect for the other. Rapists do not love their victims. How, then, can we understand Shechem's apparent change of attitude?

One option is to cast doubt on the positive connotations of the description of Shechem's behavior toward Dinah. The phrase "his soul was drawn to Dinah" is, indeed, not so spiritual as it may sound in English. Since the "soul" is understood as the seat of emotions, including passion, to say that Shechem's soul "was drawn to" or "remained close to" Dinah may imply that he continued to desire her as a sexual object. Following in this line of thinking, the next verb should not be translated "love," but "desire," to do with as he pleases, and Shechem's "tender" speech is an attempt to break down Dinah's defenses. Shechem, the prince, intends to keep the object of his desire, and Dinah is in jeopardy of becoming little more than the prince's sex slave.

Another possibility is to accept the unlikely premise that Shechem did indeed violate Dinah, acting without regard for her well-being, but that he has now come to love her and be concerned for her welfare. The words used to describe his actions have strong positive connotations in other contexts, including contexts of courtship and marriage. Interestingly, Shechem's offer to marry Dinah is perfectly in line with the requirements of Deuteronomy 22:28–29, in which a man who has sex with an unbetrothed woman (without specifying whether the woman agreed to the act) must pay her father the bride-price and marry her.

What is the outcome for Dinah if she casts her lot with this foreigner whose behavior toward her has thus far been inconsistent? We must acknowledge, however painfully, that she has few options. Her status in her family is irreparably damaged, and she is unlikely to be taken as anyone else's bride. Better for her to place her hopes in the one who, alone in the narrative, at least regards her as "Jacob's daughter."

Those who argue that Dinah and Shechem's relationship was consensual find this part of the text to be powerful evidence for their reading. While their first encounter may have been sudden or unexpected, these readers say, it was not a violation of Dinah's ability to determine the use of her own body. Of all the male characters in the story, Shechem alone deals with Dinah first as a person, and only secondarily as an item of property. Dinah and Shechem's flouting of social propriety serves to reveal the shallowness of the system and its disregard for women as human persons.

Male Wrangling

> And Hamor the father of Shechem went out to Jacob
> to speak with him, just as the sons of Jacob came in
> from the field. (34:6–7a)

Dramatic tension in the story increases still further as Hamor, Shechem, and all of Dinah's male relatives arrive simultaneously at Jacob's tent. Jacob, we are told in verse 5, already knows that Dinah and Shechem have had sex, but the narrative gives no clue as to Jacob's attitude toward this news. He "held his peace." Does this mean that Jacob, like his daughter, is open to the possibility of closer relationships with his foreign neighbors and is ready to hear what sort of alliance this might be? Or should Jacob be read as weak and vacillating, deferring to his sons, unable to take definitive action on his own? This story appears two chapters after Jacob's encounter with the mysterious man at Peniel, which left him with a physical disability. Perhaps the distance between father and daughter implied by the first verse of the chapter resurfaces here, and Jacob's inaction betrays his apathy.

Much of our judgment regarding Jacob's response is likely to stem from our own attitude regarding inaction. If we understand inaction as a sign of weakness, we are likely to judge Jacob harshly. If, however, we see inaction as unwillingness to enter the cycle of violence and as seeking a path of peace, we will sympathize with Jacob's silence and regret that his calmer demeanor does not prevail.

In sharp contrast to their father, Dinah's brothers respond immediately, with strong sentiment, to the news of Dinah and Shechem's liaison. The brothers' emotion does not seem to stem from sympathy for the experience of their sister or from their emotional attachment to her. Rather, they are angry at what they see as a "reckless act" on the part of Shechem: namely, lying with Dinah (without a word about any force Shechem may or may not have employed). Presumably some other "reckless act" could have angered them as easily. Even when the brothers have taken their revenge and are reprimanded by Jacob, their response does not reflect their concern for Dinah's feelings: "Should our sister be treated like a [prostitute]?" (v. 31). As numerous commentators have pointed out, a prostitute is not raped. Whatever happened to Dinah, her brothers' concern seems to be entirely for familial honor as it is represented by their sister's body, not for her perception of the experience.

Yet the brothers' self-centered attitude should caution us not to assume, based entirely on their response, that Dinah did not experience force or that she entered into the liaison with Shechem willingly (like a prostitute, from the brothers' point of view). To them, her experience is immaterial. Here is some of the clearest evidence that this story is no longer about Dinah herself. A sexual event has become a political event, and a political event is part of the world of men, not of women. Dinah is a pawn, a bargaining chip, as a fertile field or a freshwater spring might be. The men's negotiations quickly move beyond the matter of Dinah's possible marriage to Shechem and into the wider realm of political alliances and economic advantage.

The motive of Shechem and Hamor in offering a generous bride-price for Dinah is a crucial question. Are they acting honorably, even if their action is understood as a move to restore honor that has been inappropriately taken? Or are they continuing to dishonor Jacob's family with a deal made under false pretenses, perhaps with the goal of absorbing, and so eliminating, this foreign presence from their midst? They suggest to Jacob's sons that a marriage and political alliance between them would benefit the house of Jacob, opening the possibility of greater trade, which would increase Jacob's fortunes. On the other hand, their presentation to the men of the city (vv. 21–23) of the deal they have struck with Jacob notably avoids mention of Shechem's liaison with Dinah and suggests that good relations with Jacob's family will be economically advantageous for the city dwellers.

Clearly, both speeches are rhetorically crafted for their respective audiences. This discrepancy leads some readers to cry foul, arguing that the differences reveal Shechem and Hamor's deceitful motives. But not every judicious use of rhetoric is necessarily an attempt to deceive. With Jacob's family, Hamor and Shechem must put to rest the mistrust of a small group contemplating an alliance with a much larger one. Meanwhile, the men of the city must be brought to accept the prospect of painful circumcision, so Hamor and Shechem frame the situation in its best possible light.

Shechem hardly carves out a strong negotiating position for himself with regard to Jacob and his sons. He is, as Fewell and Gunn note, "opening himself up to the possibility of being 'taken to the cleaners' by Dinah's family."[1] His willingness to expose his own vulnerability is evidence against a charge of duplicity on Shechem's part.

While the Hivites' motive remains unstated, the narrator instructs us that Dinah's brothers act out of deceit (v. 13). This deceit seems to be directed initially against their father, who is unlikely to agree to their plan of revenge. If the revenge is understood as justified, their deceit might likewise be read as necessary. Nonetheless, while the possibility remains that Shechem and Hamor are dealing in good faith, the brothers' motives are at least compromised.

Simeon and Levi's Revenge

> On the third day, when they were still in pain, two of the sons of Jacob, Simeon and Levi, Dinah's brothers, took their swords and came against the city unawares, and killed all the males. (Gen. 34:25)

If it were not for the clue in verse 13 that Jacob's sons negotiated "deceitfully" with Hamor and Shechem, the reader unfamiliar with the biblical story would likely find its climax to be a shocking turn of events. Even readers who already know the story may read this passage with revulsion. In straightforward, compact language, the narrator relates how Simeon and Levi secretly attack and slaughter men incapable of defending themselves. Nor are Simeon and Levi alone in their brutality. Jacob's other sons arrive in the city in

---

[1]Dana Nolan Fewell and David M. Gunn, "Tipping the Balance: Sternberg's Reader and the Rape of Dinah," *JBL* 110.2 (1991): 201.

their brothers' wake, plundering property and the bereft survivors alike. The wives and "little ones" of the slain Hivite men become Jacob's sons' "prey." The cycle of violence, including sexual violence, spirals. The rape of one (if, indeed, it was rape to begin with) becomes the indisputable rape of a multitude.

Jacob, who has not acted before now, is roused to anger against his sons. "You have brought trouble on me by making me odious to the inhabitants of the land, the Canaanites and the Perizzites; my numbers are few, and if they gather themselves against me and attack me, I shall be destroyed, both I and my household" (v. 30). Again, Jacob's motives are difficult to discern. Is he a weak and self-centered man who cares little for his daughter but at least is able to sense a threat to himself? Or should we hear the anguished lament of a would-be peacemaker who has been unable to stop the cycle of violence and now fears its continuation? It is worth noting that Jacob speaks both of himself and of his "household." Jacob remains the *paterfamilias*, responsible for the well-being not only of males capable of defending themselves but also of women and children. His priorities are likely to be different than those of his hotheaded sons, who have enriched themselves by violent means.

Simeon and Levi are unrepentant: "Should our sister be treated like a [prostitute]?" (v. 31). As we have already noted, their comment, taken at face value, would weigh in on the side of Dinah's not having been raped, but having invited illicit sexual activity. Shechem's offense, by this reckoning, would be that of assuming that Dinah, like a prostitute, is capable of independent consent regarding her own body. That is, she is not part of a family structure, since in the ancient world the family's consent, not the individual's, was what mattered. Dinah's brothers claim, in effect, that Shechem has acted as if they, her family, did not exist. For this insult, the brothers consider their violent response justified.

As we have also noted, however, the evaluation of Levi and Simeon cannot be taken as a reliable indicator of Dinah's experience, or even of their knowledge of Dinah's point of view. The offense is to their own honor, as they understand themselves to represent the family. The whole incident suggests the culmination of a series of previous, unnarrated disputes. In *The Red Tent* Diamant's Dinah suggests accusations of swindling and refusal of hospitality: "My brother had been dispatched to see when I would be sent home, and had he been given a fine meal and a bed for the night, my life might have had a different telling" (*Red Tent*, 192). However the animosity began, though, by the time of this incident it has escalated past the possibility of peaceful resolution.

In the midst of this narrative of violence, the reader may be startled to discover that Simeon and Levi "took Dinah out of Shechem's house" (v. 26). We suddenly realize that Dinah has been in Shechem's house since the second verse of the narrative, physically absent from "her" story. If we are still inclined to think of Shechem as violent and deceitful, and his protestations of love as inauthentic, we may breathe a sigh of relief that in the midst of all this brutality at least Dinah is rescued from her captors. If, however, we have come to understand Shechem and Dinah's relationship as a loving one, the brothers' behavior toward their sister is yet another part of the mayhem they inflict on the inhabitants of the city. Even if Dinah's initial encounter with Shechem was against her wishes, with his stated willingness to keep her as his wife, remaining with him might have been in Dinah's best interests, given her quite limited alternatives.[2]

But although it is unclear whether Shechem has taken Dinah by her own choice, there is no lack of clarity regarding Simeon and Levi's action. They take Dinah without consideration of her choice. At best they choose for her a life of marginality and rejection. At worst, as Diamant's Dinah narrates, their murderous rampage destroys everything Dinah held dear, including her relationship with the family to whom they return her.

---

[2]Fewell and Gunn acknowledge that this option is problematic: "To advocate a woman's marrying her rapist might itself seem to be a dangerous and androcentric advocacy. And so it would be if the story world offered other liberating alternatives.

But for there to be a whole other way there would have to be a whole other world" (ibid., 211).

Conclusion

The Bible is written from a male perspective. Most of its main characters are males, and women are generally identified by their relationship with men. They are someone's wife, someone's mother, someone's daughter, someone's sister. Their stories, when they catch the limelight, are narrated briefly. Often the narrator's concern seems focused on the outcome of events for the men connected to the woman, rather than for the woman herself.

Dinah's story, though, is remarkable for the level of indeterminacy of the narrative. In the episode narrated in Genesis 34, it is unusually difficult to determine the chain of events, the motivations of the various characters, or the characters' attitudes toward Dinah. This is a story about boundaries, about honor and shame, about political relations with one's foreign neighbors, about the way insider and outsider status are defined. It is not, at least primarily, about what happened to Dinah. Readers who want to pursue the question of Dinah's experience find that they must read the text against the grain.

Nor are the difficulties of reading this story confined to determining its true subject matter. The question of how Dinah experienced the narrated events must be considered in light of questions of ancient self-understanding, how individuals in the ancient world perceived themselves, their identity, and their place in society. Too often we presume that ideals such as individualism and self-determination are part of the universal human spirit, when in fact they are ways of thinking that developed only fairly recently in the history of civilization. Such a modern viewpoint would have been impossible for Dinah—or for Shechem, Hamor, or Jacob. Their ways of understanding themselves and their places in society fundamentally differ from ours, or from those we may impose on them.

Was Dinah raped? One way to expose the difficulty of the question is to consider the different ways rape is understood in the biblical texts and today. What makes an act of sexual intercourse rape? Today the definition has to do with the use or threat of force and the lack of the woman's consent. As Sandie Gravett points out, such a definition presumes a woman's right to determine the sexual boundaries of her own body. In the Hebrew Bible, an act of sexual intercourse is considered rape (whichever Hebrew word is used to describe it) if it involves the theft of sexual property. As such, rape is an offense against the person to whom a woman's sexuality belongs, and not against the woman herself. From this vantage point, of course, Dinah was raped. Her father, who is responsible for safeguarding her sexuality, does not sanction her encounter with Shechem beforehand. But while this answer helps us understand the world of the biblical text, we do not hear Dinah's own voice in it.

The notion that a woman's sexuality can be the property of another person is foreign to us, perhaps so much so that we have trouble even imagining it. Consider, then, this contemporary analogy. An adult who performs sex acts with a minor can be prosecuted for statutory rape. This crime, according to our justice system, is committed even if the minor willingly participates in the act, because our society has determined that persons under a certain age do not qualify as "consenting adults." One way of thinking of ancient society, then, is to point out that women simply lack an "age of consent." A woman who is part of a family is never considered capable of making independent decisions about her sexuality, so judgment about an unauthorized sexual encounter does not take her volition into account.

It may be argued that this is another way of saying that women in the ancient world were less than fully human—at least, that all women were regarded as less than free adult males. Women's general lack of voice in the biblical narratives, their primary identification with male relatives, and their frequent anonymity also point in this direction. But texts do not dictate their own interpretation, and we are free to query these texts for answers that are not immediately forthcoming. Whether we find here Dinah the rape survivor, Dinah the lover of Shechem, or Dinah who struggles with uncomfortable options until even those are snatched away from her, we are free to insist on paying attention to Dinah herself, though the movement of the biblical text is in the direction of overlooking her. Whatever the particulars of her story, we recognize that here is a woman who has suffered great pain and survived. We are eager to give her voice to tell the tale.

QUESTIONS FOR DISCUSSION

1. What do you understand to be the attitude of the biblical narrator toward Dinah? Why?
2. What is particularly powerful about this biblical text if Dinah is read as a rape survivor? What is particularly powerful about this biblical text if Dinah is read as Shechem's lover by her own choice?
3. What difference does it make to the story that Shechem is a member of the ruling social class?
4. How do you perceive Jacob's role in the incident? Is he a weakling, a man of peace, or does he simply not care about his daughter?
5. How have women's roles changed since the society depicted in the biblical narrative? In what instances do you still see signs of women being slighted or devalued today?

For Further Reading

Bechtel, Lyn M. "What If Dinah Is Not Raped? (Genesis 34)." *Journal for the Study of the Old Testament* 62, no. 1 (June 1994): 19–36.

Brenner, Athalya. *I Am…: Biblical Women Tell Their Own Stories.* Minneapolis: Fortress Press, 2005.

Fewell, Danna Nolan, and David M. Gunn, "Tipping the Balance: Sternberg's Reader and the Rape of Dinah." *Journal of Biblical Literature* 110, no. 2 (Summer 1991): 193–211.

Frymer-Kensky, Tikva. *Reading the Women of the Bible: A New Interpretation of Their Stories*. New York: Schocken Books, 2002.

Gravett, Sandie. "Reading 'Rape' in the Hebrew Bible: A Consideration of Language." *Journal for the Study of the Old Testament* 28, no. 3 (March 2004): 279–99.

Scholz, Susanne. "Through Whose Eyes? A 'Right' Reading of Genesis 34." In *Genesis*, The Feminist Companion to the Bible (Second Series), edited by Athalya Brenner, 150–71. Sheffield, Eng.: Sheffield Academic Press, 1998.

Sheres, Ita. *Dinah's Rebellion: A Biblical Parable for Our Time*. New York: Crossroad, 1990.

CHAPTER 2

Discovering Dinah

> *If you want to understand any woman you must first ask about her mother and then listen carefully. Stories about food show a strong connection. Wistful silences demonstrate unfinished business. The more a daughter knows the details of her mother's life—without flinching or whining—the stronger the daughter.*
>
> (*Red Tent*, 2)

> *Jacob settled in the land where his father had lived as an alien, the land of Canaan. This is the story of the family of Jacob.*
>
> (Gen. 37:1–2a)

The stories of Jacob's family, like the other patriarchal narratives (Genesis 12—50), circulated orally for centuries before being written in the form that has come down to us. Those who told these stories, and those who recorded them in writing, had particular reasons for doing so—not always the reasons we read the texts today. These stories were not recorded to offer future readers insight into the daily lives of the women in the narratives. To uncover details of their existence, then, we must use carefully the various historical tools at our disposal and ask thoughtful questions about the evidence we find.

Dating the Patriarchs

Rarely does an orally transmitted story contain any suggestion as to its date. Even if it mentions a ruler or other known personage, often the information is too general to be helpful: *which* Egyptian pharaoh, for example, is the Pharaoh of the exodus? In similar manner it is often difficult to tell which details of oft-repeated stories are historical data and which have passed into the realm of legend. Embroidered with legendary details, the stories may tell us a great deal about how the successive generations of storytellers perceived their subject, but less about what that person actually said or did on a given occasion.

A contemporary storyteller who wishes to base her imaginative retelling on a biblical text and historical evidence must choose a historical setting for her story so that she can use historical information from other sources to fill out the details the biblical text does not supply. Diamant apparently chose the most typically asserted dates for Jacob's family, during the Middle Bronze Age, ca. 1900 B.C.E. This is a period during which worship of goddesses was still strong and widespread. Another theory for the dating of the historical Jacob is at the beginning of the Iron Age, ca. 1100 B.C.E. This seems less likely for Diamant's reconstruction, as by this time goddesses were much less important in many ancient religious systems.

What Mean These Stones?

Written texts are not the only way we gain insight into ancient cultures. Archeology offers us a window into the material culture and, often, the social practices of ancient societies. Archeologists uncover architectural structures, trash heaps, burial places, and other evidence of ancient human life. Contemporary archeologists discover evidence of women as well as men, infants and children as well as adults, the ordinary as well as the well-to-do.

Yet archeology also presents a set of challenges. Artifacts, like texts, must be "read." Is this small figurine a religious item or a child's plaything? Was this item destroyed because it was unwanted or defective, or because it was ritually broken? Did this mace-shaped implement flay the skin of an animal to prepare leather, or crush grain to make bread? Objects do not tell us their intended use, and researchers from a very different cultural context are likely to misidentify objects based on their own experiences. Nor do objects tell us who used them, so often we cannot determine the sexual division of labor by archeology alone.

Major digs usually focus on architectural ruins, which means that we learn more about settled peoples than about nomads. City walls and the walls of houses leave ruins; tents do not, and even the burial grounds and trash piles of a settlement comprising primarily tents are likely to be obliterated or simply lost to future generations.

The city of Shechem has been excavated, and archeologists have some idea about when it was inhabited, the periods in which it was uninhabited (or sparsely inhabited), and when it was strongly fortified. Nonetheless, researchers cannot say with certainty why the city went through its various cycles of flourishing and abandonment, with the exception of an event in the latter part of the Middle Bronze Age, in which the city was attacked, looted, torn down, and burned, with bodies thrown out into the street. This destruction almost certainly was the result of an attack by Egyptian armies during a time of Egyptian expansion into the Canaanite region. If, indeed, there were a raid on the location now identified as Shechem by a group of attackers such as Jacob's family, it would have to have happened during one of the times when the city was relatively small and its walls were not strongly fortified.

Archeologists, and those who hope to discover new information about the past from the work of archeologists, must work to keep their own expectations or wishes about what they hope to find from inappropriately determining their conclusions. At the same time, they must remain genuinely open to the possibilities that ancient societies may have functioned very differently from societies today.

Looking for the Women

Few ancient texts tell us about women's experience, and even fewer about their daily lives. Texts in a woman's own voice are rarer still. Archeology yields items of daily life that can give us some information about what women did and how they did it. Spindles and whorls are often found in women's graves, reinforcing the impression that the production of cloth was women's work. In *The Red Tent*, Dinah mentions burying a spindle and an alabaster bowl with Meryt. Combs and other hair adornments can generally be assumed to be women's property too, and what is found with them, even in refuse piles, is often understood to be the stuff of women's lives.

Yet such items are often trivial, except perhaps to the researcher vitally interested in the technological developments behind the production of cloth, or as an indication of the technical skill of the civilization indexed in the intricacy and accuracy of carving or metalwork on a comb or bangle. Of greater interest to those of us who would like to know how ancient women understood their relationship to the divine are various statues, typically of pottery, that represent the female figure. These "pillar-figurines" depict an apparently naked woman from the waist up; the lower body is a pillar that flares at the base to allow the figure to stand. Typically the breasts of such figures are prominent, and often the figure's hands are placed under the breasts, likely emphasizing the nurture of the nursing mother. But like many archeological artifacts, further interpretation of these figures is problematic. Do they represent a goddess, and if so, which one? Some scholars have argued that they are unlikely goddess-figures, because they are of ordinary material, plain and unadorned with the symbols that usually represent deity. They are more probably votary figures, the physical representation of women's prayers and hopes for successful pregnancy, childbirth, and lactation. In any case, they are material evidence of the religious practice of ordinary women whose lives are all but invisible to us from textual sources.

Valuing Women's Work

We are socialized to think of the tasks of housekeeping and childrearing both as "woman's work" (although we may chafe at the designation) and as less valuable than other kinds of work. Certainly our market economy places less value on the work of cleaning houses or working in a child-care center than it does on financial management, the practice of medicine, or jobs in manufacturing. To the extent that these latter fields have often been understood as male domain, they represent a piece of the male-dominated system that keeps women in subjugated roles.

From such a perspective, we may think of women in the ancient world as more completely subjugated than women in the modern era. After all, their entire lives were focused on domestic labor: keeping a household and rearing children. They were typically afforded no education beyond their domestic role, and they rarely interacted with persons outside the family structure. They were treated, we are told, as property by their fathers/husbands/male guardians, and if they experienced ill treatment, they lacked legal recourse.

Yet if we step back from our contemporary perspective, we may discern that the categories we use to define women's "subjugation" are not appropriate for the ancient world. While we may think of domestic labor as stultifying, for the household-based subsistence economies of the ancient world such labor was the core expression of civilization. Turning wool (or flax) into clothing to cover human nakedness or raw grain into bread and beer to satisfy human hunger and thirst—these transformations were wrought by the labor of women. The manufacture of most of the products required to meet the household's needs was domestic work, performed primarily by women. (Sometimes men made pottery, and metallurgy was typically a men's task, but a typical agrarian household would have used very few metal items.) Women also collected or tended herbs and medicinal

preparations and managed the household stores of pro-
visions, which were a family's primary wealth. Senior females
directed the activities of younger women, and probably of
younger males as well. Thus the economics of an agrarian
household such as Jacob's did not function in the same way
as a modern market economy based on larger political
systems. Far from being economically marginalized,
women's work was specialized, skilled, and essential to the
family's survival.

We see the household economics of Jacob's family from
this woman-centered perspective. In *The Red Tent*, Leah is
the household manager as well as the person in charge of
food preparation. Before she is married to Jacob, she functions
as the manager of Laban's household. Her superior
knowledge of Laban's herds and flocks is attributed in part
to Laban's shiftlessness. Nonetheless, it is to her that Jacob
looks to learn what he needs to know about Laban's livestock
holdings, though the actual tasks of animal husbandry were
men's work. On various occasions the reader learns that Leah
controls the stores of food. She is the one who plans and
prepares the grand meal when Jacob first arrives at Laban's
tents, as she recalls: "Nobody helped me with the cooking,
not that I would have permitted anyone else to touch the
lamb or the bread, or even the barley water. I wouldn't let
my own mother pour water into a pot" (*Red Tent*, 17). When
Leah wishes to make a celebration, the entire household
feasts. If she is out of sorts, they must make do with barley
porridge.

Other women of the household also have particular roles
in food production. Some of Rachel's herbs season the
vegetables. Bilhah makes dried-goat stew seasoned with fresh
onions, to the displeasure of Esau's Canaanite wife. The
women work together in the garden and grind the grain.
These tasks reflect the central importance of female labor.
Although Jacob's family is represented as being relatively
prosperous, daily necessities are not acquired in trade, but
produced within the household by its women. Without their
labor, the household could not function as an economic unit.

As with foodstuffs, the agrarian household as economic unit produced its own clothing. Cloth was also an important item of trade, since it was portable and represented a significant amount of labor. Men participated by breeding and tending the sheep and by shearing the fleece. From that point on, women did the washing, carding, spinning, and weaving, as well as the production of articles of clothing from whole cloth. Both genders, then, performed important tasks to the provision of bodily coverings, but the women's work was essential if people were not simply going to cover themselves with skins, but were going to wear garments fashioned of cloth.

All the women in *The Red Tent* participate in spinning and weaving, though Zilpah and Bilhah are particularly accomplished, weaving the multicolored wool into beautiful patterns for trade. Dinah comments that she is not particularly skilled with the spindle and that weaving is a task more difficult than she imagined. Yet she is rarely without a spindle to work wool into thread, even when the family is traveling. One of the first acts of settling in a new place is to set up the large and cumbersome, but necessary, looms.

While tasks in ancient societies were largely segregated by gender, women's work was no less important than the work done by men. For the agrarian economy, the work done by women—childrearing, food preparation, the manufacture of clothing, and the like—was neither devalued nor marginalized, but absolutely central to the way society functioned.

Women's Seclusion, Women's Leisure

Women's full participation in the economic life of their families did not put them on an equal social footing with men. Ancient Mesopotamian and Canaanite society was undoubtedly patriarchal, and men seem to have regarded women as the necessary, yet potentially dangerous, "Other." Part of women's "Otherness" and "dangerousness" stemmed no doubt from their power of procreation. Although ancient people understood that the male had a role in procreation, it was the woman who conceived or failed to conceive. This society often found it impossible to discern the circumstances that caused one woman to bear one healthy child after another, another woman to experience multiple miscarriages and stillbirths, and yet another woman to be completely barren. In times of scarce resources in particular (and these were frequent in the ancient world), a woman's fertility could mean the difference between continuation and obliteration of the family line.

Women in their childbearing years, and thus women potentially capable of producing new life, also did something mysterious and possibly dangerous: they bled, every month, from between their legs. Ancients did not know the medical details of the female reproductive cycle, but they were well aware that this monthly blood flow had to do with women's capacity to bear children. In addition, in many ancient cultures blood was understood as a source of ritual pollution. A woman's menstrual blood, predictable yet mysterious, issuing from a woman but not seeming to sap her strength, somehow associated with her childbearing ability—this blood was a source of impurity, and various means were devised to mark it as such. In the Israelite tradition, part of the law understood to be given to Moses on Sinai addressed the uncleanness of menstrual blood:

> When a woman has a discharge of blood that is her regular discharge from her body, she shall be in her impurity for seven days, and whoever touches her shall be unclean until the evening. Everything upon which she lies during her impurity shall be unclean; everything also upon which she sits shall be unclean. Whoever touches her bed shall wash his clothes, and bathe in water, and be unclean until the evening. Whoever touches anything upon which she sits shall wash his clothes, and bathe in water, and be unclean until the evening; whether it is the bed or anything upon which she sits, when he touches it he shall be unclean until the evening. If any man lies with her, and her impurity falls on him, he shall be unclean seven days; and every bed on which he lies shall be unclean. (Lev. 15:19–24)

Other societies, too, pronounced limitations on menstruants. Some legal codes sought to proscribe a woman from baking bread or certain other household tasks during her period.

Yet these regulations seem to have been honored more in legislation than in practice. The Pentateuchal narratives surrounding the giving of the law assume that the tabernacle is in the midst of the community, so uncleanness concerns are paramount. By the time these texts were compiled, in the exilic and postexilic periods, many Israelites did not have regular access to the temple in Jerusalem, and ritual uncleanness was not a central concern for many common people. While archeological records, as we have noted, are scarce or nonexistent for tent-dwellers, evidence from settled towns does not indicate sufficient space in ordinary homes for women to be secluded on a regular basis, even in societies that expressed uneasiness about women's menstrual uncleanness. We have some evidence that women workers in cities received days off at the time of their period, but this comes from several centuries later than our era of interest and from an urban society in which women were more or less interchangeable workers, not an agrarian family unit in which each individual's contribution was essential to the whole.

Thus it is unlikely, from a historical perspective, that a family group in Middle Bronze Age Mesopotamian agrarian societies would have had a "red tent" for the purpose of housing menstruating women in seclusion. Women living together in all likelihood experienced very similar menstrual cycles, and it is not unimaginable that they performed a ceremony to welcome the new moon. Such a ceremony is documented in ancient societies, and some contemporary Jewish feminists have advocated revitalizing the practice of Rosh Hodesh, "new month," with a women's liturgy that includes dance, song, and the breaking of bread together. The story of Jephthah's daughter probably preserves traces of women's coming-of-age ceremonies that involved time spent away from the family group (Judg. 11:7–38). But three days for rest and repose out of each month, as attractive as it may be as a religious practice that affirms women's spirituality, would almost certainly not have been possible in a family such as that of Jacob. The work done by women was too essential to the family's functioning to spare. The red tent, powerful image as it is, comes from the fictional part of Diamant's historical fiction.

Yet it should not discourage us to recognize that Diamant has taken elements from the biblical text—a complicated female family dynamic, a lone daughter among a horde of brothers, and a biblical story about a woman whose voice is never heard—and combined them with both historical evidence and her novelist's imagination to create a compelling narrative that speaks to us today. *The Red Tent* is, after all, an imaginative retelling, not just a recounting of history. Through the literary device of the red tent, Diamant draws together elements of the story that would be disparate and scattered in any other method of retelling. She makes it possible for us, as contemporary readers, to enter into the story, as we imagine ourselves, too, in the red tent that she sets up for her characters.

The Facts of Life

One historical aspect of ordinary life that Diamant's novel conveys vividly and with sensitivity is the awareness that death was an ever-present reality, often claiming infants, children, and adults—especially childbearing women—in the prime of life. One of the characteristics that Diamant's Dinah attributes to modern women is that we are "so safe in childbed" (*Red Tent*, 3). In ancient times a woman's journey from conception through childbearing was fraught with uncertainty, danger, and pain.

Inability to conceive a child was attributed to the woman; she was considered "barren." A man could be disgraced by his wife's barrenness, just as he received honor when she bore a child; but the inadequacy of the husband's "seed" was not seen as the reason for a couple's inability to produce a child. Women who were unable to become pregnant were encouraged to try a variety of remedies, as we see with Rachel:

> Rachel tried every remedy, every potion, every rumored cure. She wore only red and yellow—the colors of life's blood and the talisman for healthy menstruation. She slept with her belly against trees said to be sacred to local goddesses. Whenever she saw running water, she lay down in it, hoping for the life of the river to inspire life within her. She swallowed a tincture made with bee pollen until her tongue was coated yellow and she peed a saffron river. She dined upon snake—the animal that gives birth to itself, year after year. (*Red Tent*, 46–47)

Rachel tries mandrakes as well, and the rest of the family helps, bringing to her every root they find. Incantations, herbal concoctions, votive offerings, charms and amulets, these rituals all seemed to work for some women and to fail with others. Ultimately, many believed, only the gods could open or close a woman's womb.

Of course, a fertile woman had reasons not to become pregnant. Dinah mentions the beeswax pessary and the fennel seeds that Leah uses as birth control measures after bearing four sons in short order. Her cousin Tabea hopes to become a priestess or an acolyte rather than a wife, because she does not want to experience the pain of childbirth or the loss of infant children. On occasion, too, a woman might seek to abort a developing pregnancy. Midwives, skilled in the use of all sorts of herbs, were generally assumed to know how to abort a fetus, as Rachel does for Ruti. Many of the herbal drinks that ancient women used as oral contraceptives were likely also abortifacients if conception had already taken place. Intentional abortion was risky, not only to the health of the woman, but also because of the legal consequences it could entail. In many ancient cultures, a woman who aborted her child was punished by death, and anyone found to have assisted her could be liable as well.

Once the child was conceived, concern for its well-being immediately set in. Miscarriages were common, likely due to a variety of factors: poor maternal nutrition, various forms of illness (chronic diseases often went undiagnosed), a mother who was too young or insufficiently recovered from a previous pregnancy loss. Ancients often attributed miscarriage to evil spirits, inadequate protection by the deities that were thought to look after expectant mothers, sorcery, or plain bad luck—which was also often attributed to the gods. Pregnant women frequently wore amulets to guard against miscarriage, typically with particular stones thought to have power to protect the fetus from harm.

When a woman's time came to give birth, her female relatives or neighbors and the midwife assisted in the labor itself and offered encouragement and comfort to the laboring mother. Massaging with oil was common, around the perineum to help it stretch, and on the mother's body to relax her and make her pain more bearable. Incantations and songs invited the gods to bless the birth and reassured the laboring woman that she was following in a long line of mothers before her. Often these incantations imaged the infant about to be born as a boat or barge traveling down the birth canal, sometimes steered by Inanna, Ninhursag, or another of the mother goddesses. At other times the incantations would call on the infant to slip out like a snake, surely a hopeful thought to a woman frantic with worry lest her hips be too narrow to allow her child to pass through.

As is clear from Dinah's descriptions, in the ancient world, delivery itself was typically accomplished by crouching or squatting, with the legs supported by bricks or blocks. A woman exhausted by long labor would, of course, need support to attain the squatting position. The midwife knelt in front of the laboring woman and caught the infant, usually in a blanket, as it emerged. She suctioned its nose and mouth if necessary, tied off the umbilical cord, and disposed of the afterbirth or wrapped it for ritual handling.

In contemporary practice, caesarean sections are performed for a number of reasons: when labor has gone on an unusually long time or has stalled and cannot be induced to resume; when fetal distress is detected; when the mother's health is endangered by high blood pressure or some other mishap; when serious infection is present or suspected; when the infant is judged too large, or the mother too small, for successful vaginal delivery; when the infant is not correctly positioned for vaginal delivery; or for a number of other reasons. Today this procedure is performed under sterile surgical conditions, and nearly always both child and mother survive and recover.

In the ancient world, all the same complications could arise, but the women had far fewer attractive options. Herbs and medicinal preparations could induce stalled labor. Sometimes a skilled midwife could turn an infant into a more appropriate position for delivery. Dinah directs Meryt to perform an episiotomy, a procedure apparently unknown to the Egyptian midwife, to allow Re-mose to be born. But frequently labor complications were beyond the ability of the midwife to remedy, and either the mother or the child, or both, died. A stillbirth could still be delivered, although in such instances the mother's grief and despair might cause her to lose the will to live. But when a dead mother's body held a still-living child, the knowledgeable midwife might perform the ancient version of a caesarean, cutting the dead woman open to free the infant. Dinah learns this procedure from Inna, but discovers that it is unknown among the midwives she encounters in Egypt, who seem to assume that taking a knife to the human body is the province of (male) surgeons alone.

After a baby was born, the umbilical cord was tied and cut—an important moment, since it represented the independence of the child from its mother, and a likely time to offer prayers and incantation to ward off diseases and evil spirits, and seek for the child a propitious fate. The infant was washed, sometimes rubbed with salt, and swaddled. As soon as possible, it was placed at its mother's breast to nurse. As we see in *The Red Tent*, sometimes an exhausted or ill mother would lose consciousness after birth, so nursing might be delayed, or the infant might nurse, temporarily or permanently, from another woman. The role of wet nurse was an important one, since maternal illness and death were common, and since in some ancient cultures upper-class women were not expected to nurse their own children. A number of ancient documents deal with the employment of wet nurses:

the need for a wet nurse to be a person of good character (since she would spend a great deal of time with the young child), the pay she should receive, the expectations written into wet-nursing contracts that the wet nurse should not become pregnant or take more than one child to nurse during the contract period.

At times, of course, infants were born with birth defects. The standard procedure for such cases, death by exposure, seems cruel and heartless to us, but we must take into account the impossibility of corrective or reconstructive surgery to repair defects. Such births were also seen as a bad omen or curse for the family, and rituals existed to rid a person or household of the evil that a malformed birth portended. Most interesting to us, perhaps, are the cases of unusual features that did not affect bodily function, as with Leah's eyes—one blue, one green. Dinah reports that the infant Leah's eyes cause some to suspect her of being or harboring an evil spirit. Even the midwife recommends that she be drowned at once, to keep evil from entering the family. There is no mandate, however, to determine what must be done with such an infant, and despite his general superstition Laban chooses to raise the child.

Conclusion

The Red Tent draws on bits of historical knowledge we have about the ancient world to paint a vivid picture of life in a setting very different from our own. Diamant's characters are powerfully drawn, not only because their setting possesses historical verisimilitude, but also because they are the products of the novelist's creative imagination. Knowing more about the historical background, and the limits of our historical knowledge, helps us appreciate the accomplishment that brings Diamant's characters to life.

QUESTIONS FOR DISCUSSION

---

1. Why is it difficult to derive information about women's daily lives from ancient texts and archeological finds?

2. Does the realization that women's work was skilled and essential to the survival of the family change the way you think about the role of women in the ancient world?
3. How does the literary device of the red tent organize and shape Diamant's narrative?
4. How does an understanding of childbirth in ancient times enhance your reading of the novel, particularly with regard to Dinah's role as a midwife?

For Further Reading

Bird, Phyllis. *Missing Persons and Mistaken Identities: Women and Gender in Ancient Israel.* Minneapolis: Fortress Press, 1997.

Meyers, Carol. *Discovering Eve: Ancient Israelite Women in Context.* New York: Oxford Univ. Press, 1988.

———. *Households and Holiness: The Religious Culture of Israelite Women.* Facets Series. Minneapolis: Fortress Press, 2005.

Schottroff, Luise, Silvia Schroer, and Marie-Theres Wacker, *Feminist Interpretation: The Bible in Women's Perspective.* Translated by Martin and Barbara Rumscheidt. Minneapolis: Fortress Press, 1998.

Stol, M. *Birth in Babylonia and the Bible: Its Mediterranean Setting.* Cuneiform Monographs 14. Groningen: Styx Publications, 2000.

CHAPTER 3

Reading Texts, Filling Gaps

> *It is terrible how much has been forgotten, which is why,*
> *I suppose, remembering seems a holy thing.*
>
> (*Red Tent,* 3)

> *Keep these words that I am commanding you today in*
> *your heart. Recite them to your children and talk about them*
> *when you are at home and when you are away, when you lie*
> *down and when you rise. Bind them as a sign on your hand,*
> *fix them as an emblem on your forehead, and write them on*
> *the doorposts of your house and on your gates.*
>
> (Deut. 6:6–9)

For many readers, *The Red Tent* at first appears to be a work of historical fiction like many others with which we are familiar. An author chooses a character from religious tradition or the annals of history, often one about whom little is recorded, and makes that character the central figure of a narrative that reflects known details about the period and adds material from the author's own imagination. Or an author chooses an important moment in time and invents a leading character, making that character plausible by involving her or him in known historical events. Whether the resulting work is *Gone With the Wind* or the latest paperback romance, placing a fictional or fictionalized story in a recognized historical era is a popular writing technique. Diamant's novel, however, is more than simply an imaginative retelling of a set of sparsely narrated biblical stories. *The Red Tent* stands in a Jewish interpretive tradition known as *midrash*, a dialogue with the biblical texts that stretches back to ancient times. To gain perspective on Diamant's version of Dinah's story, then, it is helpful for us to consider how midrash works, and what the midrashim (plural of midrash) through the ages have had to say about the stories of Dinah and her family.

What Is Midrash?

Midrash, most simply put, means interpretation. Midrash refers either to the process of interpretation ("she is doing *midrash*") or its product ("that book is a *midrash*"). The English word itself is a loan-word from Hebrew, derived from the verb *darash*, "to care about, examine, demand, seek." A midrash, then, is an interpretation, and in particular a Jewish interpretation, of a Hebrew text.

But this basic definition glosses over much of what is most important in the midrashic tradition. First, midrash is not the interpretation of just any texts, but specifically of the biblical texts, texts fraught with special significance to their rabbinic interpreters and their heirs in the midrashic tradition. Midrash inquires into texts understood as divine revelation. It is a holy practice, undertaken by interpreters who regard these texts as given for our instruction.

The goal of midrash is to uncover the meanings of scripture that instruct and edify the community. Midrash is a means of connecting scripture to the contemporary community, of giving a new sense of immediacy to the stories. The midrashists, ancient or modern, believe that their task is to allow these texts to speak to today's culture.

Midrash is serious business, but it is also rightly described as a scholarly, holy game, characterized by wordplay, multiple possibilities, tenuous connections, and the like. The classic midrashic texts are likely to startle readers accustomed to modes of Christian theological discourse. Typically they are arranged as the record of discussions among scholars and rabbis, though in actuality the individuals represented may span several centuries. No summarizing comments tell the reader which viewpoint to adopt. The overall effect, then, is one of almost dizzying variety. Many of the comments seem aimed at some connection with the midrashists' community life that most modern readers find incomprehensible, but other comments strike the reader as surprisingly apt.

Midrash as Genre

The rabbis found further meanings through a number of interpretive methods. They read words as similarly spelled words, with different vowels (in biblical Hebrew the vowels are not written in the text). They connected stories with other, entirely separate stories by means of a single keyword that appeared in both. They assumed that seemingly unrelated events must be connected if they were narrated consecutively and so developed the connections between them. They imputed motives and connected cause with effect. Perhaps most fascinating of all, they gave multiple, even contradictory, answers to the various questions they asked of the biblical texts. Thus the midrashic tradition comes down to us in a rich variety of voices.

The rabbinic materials contain two sorts of literature: *halakah*, legal discussion, and *aggadah*, narrative. *Halakah* is primarily found in texts known as the *Mishnah*, the *Tosefta*, and the Babylonian and Palestinian *Talmuds*.[1] In *halakah*, women typically appear as depersonalized types, rarely as specific persons. The midrashim focus on *aggadah*. As might be imagined, women appear in greater individuality and variety in narrative aggadic material. The retelling of stories invites the introduction of specific women in all their quirky individuality. Sometimes the rabbis judge these women, but

[1]For contemporary English editions, see Herbert Danby, trans., *The Mishnah* (London: Oxford Univ. Press, 1950); Jacob Neusner, trans., *The Tosefta* (Peabody, Mass.: Hendrickson, 2002); I. Epstein, ed., *The Babylonian Talmud* (London: Soncino Press, 1935–48); Jacob Neusner, trans., *The Talmud of the Land of Israel* (Chicago: Univ. of Chicago Press, 1982–1993).

often also praise them, even when their actions are not entirely in keeping with the rabbis' expressed ideals of feminine behavior. The midrashim uphold the virtues of modesty and traditional, home-centered roles for women. Yet these same texts exhibit tenderness for women depicted as violating traditional roles and, sometimes, pride in women leaders of the community. Midrashim thus leave open the possibility of multiple roles for women, a message well suited to contemporary women.

Midrash on the Jacob Cycle

Traditional Midrashim

The sparsely told, epic-scale accounts of Jacob and his family in the book of Genesis are precisely the sort of narratives that the rabbis sought to interpret in midrash. Since the rabbis were persuaded that the book of Genesis laid out the entire scope of Israel's history and significance, these stories, with their curious events and odd, seemingly out of place details, must mean more than at first appeared.

The fullest collection of midrash on the Jacob cycle, including the stories of Leah, Rachel, and Dinah, appears in a document known as *Genesis Rabbah*,[2] compiled around 400 C.E. from traditions that likely stretch back several generations earlier. Other texts, from the early centuries C.E. into the medieval period, make mention of these stories as well.

LEAH AND RACHEL IN THE TRADITIONAL MIDRASHIM

From the very first appearance of Laban's daughters in the Genesis narrative, we see the rabbis busily analyzing the text for deeper meanings. Is Jacob's kiss of greeting to Rachel (Gen. 29:11) improper, or an appropriate greeting among kin? Why does he weep? Is it because, unlike his father's servant going to bring Rebecca, he has no gifts of wealth to offer? Or is it because he already foresees that he and Rachel will not be buried together?

---

[2]Jacob Neusner, *Genesis Rabbah: The Judaic Commentary to the Book of Genesis: A New American Translation*, 3 vol. (Atlanta: Scholars Press, 1985).

The rabbis closely analyzed Laban's greeting to Jacob as well. Why does Laban "meet" Jacob, then "embrace" him, then "kiss" him (Gen. 29:13)? The midrashists tended to amplify what they saw as the essential character trait of each individual, and so Laban, who is revealed later in the narrative to be greedy and deceitful, was portrayed as such from the outset. Assuming that Jacob has come with a handsome bride-price for his future wife (as Eliezer brought for Rebecca), Laban first "meets" Jacob gladly. Seeing no laden camels, he "embraces" Jacob, expecting to find a hidden belt filled with gold and jewels. When this, too, proves not to be the case, Laban "kisses" Jacob, thinking that perhaps there are pearls hidden in his mouth. This detailed exegesis demonstrates the sages' own befuddlement that Jacob brought no gifts, and it explains why the text uses three verbs when presumably one would do.

One strain of speculation on the "weakness" (Gen. 29:17, NIV) of Leah's eyes said that she was promised in marriage to Esau, or that it was widely assumed that Rebecca's two sons would marry Laban's two daughters—the older to the older, the younger to the younger. Esau's bad behavior, however, caused the pious but despairing Leah to weep continuously and to pray that she would not be forced to go through with the marriage. Events, then, proved for the rabbis the power of prayer: not only was the decreed marriage to Esau averted, but Leah also married Jacob before her sister.

Jacob very clearly specifies that he intends to marry Rachel, but he finds himself married to Leah. How does such a deception take place? The rabbis offered several answers, providing further insight into their views of the main characters.

Rachel, they suggested, suspects Laban from the beginning, and she and Jacob work out a set of signs by which he can be certain that Rachel is in his bed. Yet out of love for her sister, Rachel hatches a plot of her own: she reveals the signs to Leah and even hides under the marriage bed and speaks for Leah in response to Jacob. This selfless act, the rabbis suggested, is what God "remembers" in "remembering" Rachel years later and ending her barrenness.

Another midrashic version blamed the deception squarely on Laban, though with Leah's cooperation. Laban lets his neighbors in on the plot, trying to persuade them that Jacob's continued presence among them is beneficial to all. They try to warn Jacob during the wedding festivities, shouting, "Hey, Leah, Hey, Leah," but Jacob hears their words as shouts of celebration and does not recognize the hint. All night Jacob says, "Rachel," and Leah answers to her sister's name. When in the morning Jacob indignantly reproaches Leah for answering to Rachel's name, Leah retorts: "Is there a book without readers? Your father called you 'Esau,' and you answered; you called me a name other than my own, and I answered." While contemporary readers may see in this response evidence of Leah's cleverness and clearheadedness, the ancient rabbis suggested that such an answer was the root of Jacob's hatred of Leah, such that he considers divorcing her. After God grants her sons, however, Jacob is loath to divorce the mother of his sons, and so keeps Leah as his wife.

The matter of Rachel's envy of Leah, and her sharp words to Jacob, were also of interest to the midrashists. As we have seen, the tendency was to attribute one main character trait to an individual and demonstrate how it followed through. Rachel, though, is too complicated a character in the biblical text to fit with one trait. Thus far she has been depicted as loving and compassionate to her sister, even when Leah is suspected of hypocrisy for deceiving Rachel. So how can the righteous Rachel express envy? The scribes' answer was generous to Leah and showed the beginning of a shift toward greater sympathy for Leah than for Rachel. These biases were dictated in part by the rabbis' grounding assumptions: Leah's fertility and Rachel's barrenness must mean that Leah is the more righteous woman. Thus they read the texts to impute greater uprightness to Leah, despite certain textual evidence to the contrary. Rachel, they said, envies Leah for the latter's good deeds, evidenced by her bearing children.

In the story of the mandrakes (Gen. 30:14–16), the midrashists saw Rachel as eager, perhaps too eager, to acquire the roots that are assumed to have magical properties to open the womb (though the scribes were clear that God, not a magic potion, opens the womb.) The story was interpreted to have certain resonances with Esau's sale of his birthright for the short-term gain of a meal. Rachel, they noted, indeed acquires the mandrakes, but Leah gains two sons (Issachar and Zebulun) and the right to be buried with Jacob. The rabbis interpreted Rachel's seemingly casual phrase, "he may lie with you tonight," as having significance ultimately in the matter of their burials. Leah, for her part, is judged as acting honorably despite the fact that her address to Jacob, "You must come in to me," might be construed as coarse or immodest. She acts, the rabbis said, with honorable intentions, knowing that her actions will result in more tribes for Israel.

"Afterwards," the text says—that is, after Leah has borne her sixth son, and Jacob's tenth—"she bore a daughter, and named her Dinah" (Gen. 30:21). Dinah's birth announcement is conspicuously unlike that of her brothers, the meanings of whose names are described in detail. Yet the very fact that the birth of a female child is recorded struck the scribes as noteworthy.

The matriarchs, the scribes contended, had prophetic powers. They knew (as did Jacob) that there would be twelve sons, the progenitors of twelve tribes. Leah had been surprised already at the birth of Judah, her fourth, because she had assumed that the four of them would bear three sons each. Again the scribes recognized the power of prayer. Either God anticipates Rachel's prayer after Joseph's birth, "May the LORD add to me another son!" (Gen. 30:24), or Leah herself prays that her unborn child will be a girl so that Rachel might have the opportunity to bear more than one of Jacob's sons. This, the sages said, is why Leah names the girl "Dinah" (which can mean "argue" or "judgment"); Leah "argued" with God against having a boy, or she "judged" against herself in her choice for a female child. Another version depicts the matriarchs together, rather than Leah alone, deciding that Rachel deserves more than one male child.

Leah, at least in one version of the story, is depicted as being solicitous of her sister, and God is depicted as respecting the prayers (from whatever quarter) that petition for a girl child for Leah.

The seeming connection between Dinah's birth and God's "remembering" of Rachel did not go unnoticed by the rabbis. Some argued that Joseph's conception and birth are both painless, as Sarah's delivery of Isaac is said to have been. After the births of Dinah and Joseph, the frostiness between Leah and Rachel seems to have thawed. The sisters unite with their husband against their father, Laban, who continues to be described as heartless and greedy. Together they plan to leave.

The rabbis sought an honorable motive for Rachel's theft of Laban's household gods, so they said she steals them for Laban's sake, to rid him of his idolatry. Nonetheless her action has tragic consequences. When Laban pursues Jacob and accuses him of stealing the gods, Jacob vows that anyone with whom Laban finds the gods will not live. Rachel famously pleads incapacity and refuses to rise to allow Laban to search the camel's saddle on which she sits, so that Laban does not find the gods. In one version, the figures are changed into drinking glasses, which Laban finds but does not recognize as his ritual objects. Nonetheless, the sages said, Jacob's unwitting curse is the cause, or at least one of the causes, of Rachel's untimely death.

DINAH IN THE TRADITIONAL MIDRASHIM

The portraits of Leah and Rachel that emerge in midrash are complicated and interesting ones. It is disappointing, then, to find that Dinah is one of those biblical characters that the rabbis largely summarized with a single attribute. "And Dinah...went out," begins Genesis 34:1, and it seems that the midrashists could read no further. A woman who "goes out," they argued, will come to no good end. "Like mother, like daughter," they quoted Ezekiel 16:44, although Leah "goes out" to meet her husband (Gen. 30:16) after the episode with the mandrakes for a sexual encounter that was typically described as honorable (see above). The rabbis may have seen Hamor as wicked, Shechem as an enticer and a snake, and even Jacob as careless; but on Dinah fell the ultimate blame because she is a gadabout, and such behavior is inappropriate for a woman. Uniformly, they regarded Dinah's liaison with Shechem as a violent sexual act that Dinah's inappropriate behavior brought on herself. The rabbis often imagined that a number of factors contributed to the outcome of a particular event. In Dinah's case, Jacob was seen to bear part of the responsibility for what eventually happens to her, both by his actions and by his attitudes.

Genesis 32:22 indicates that Jacob "took his two wives, his two maids, and his eleven children" across the Jabbok River. The rabbis asked: where was Dinah? She was locked in a chest, they concluded, lest Esau see her beauty and insist on taking her for his wife. Such an action, they concluded, violated scripture's prohibition against withholding kindness from a neighbor. Because Jacob did not seek to marry Dinah off in the acceptable way, to a circumcised man, she would be taken in a forbidden way, by an uncircumcised man. In the same text, the rabbis alluded to a tradition that Dinah was the wife of Job and faulted Jacob for not trying to convert him. Other traditions insisted that Dinah could have reformed Esau. Jacob's failure to offer her as a wife to Esau, then, prevented Esau from gaining a chance to turn from his evil ways.

One tradition said that Jacob failed to fulfill a vow. Another pointed to his comment to Laban, "my honesty will answer for me later" (or "tomorrow") (Gen. 30:33). Scripture, they pointed out, forbids boasting about tomorrow (Prov. 27:1); for the foolishness of this boast, "tomorrow your daughter will go out and get raped."[3]

Even though the sages judged Dinah harshly and largely blamed her for her misfortune, they were loath to leave her, despoiled and unmarried, without offspring, in her father's house for the rest of her days. As we have already mentioned,

---

[3]Ibid., 148.

one tradition made her the wife of Job because a word used to speak of Dinah's situation in Genesis 34:7 ("disgrace" or "outrage") also appears in Job 2:10 to describe Job's wife (where it is typically translated "foolish"). Another said Dinah, seen by some as the "Canaanite woman" in Genesis 46:10 because she had sexual relations with the Canaanite Shechem, marries her brother Simeon. Yet another tradition gave her a daughter by Shechem, named Asenath. Asenath is the name of Joseph's wife (Gen. 41:50), and this tradition probably intended to suggest that these two are the same. For the most part, however, Dinah served her purpose as a cautionary tale, then disappeared as completely from the midrash as she does from the text of scripture itself.

THE BURIAL OF RACHEL IN THE MIDRASH

Rachel's untimely death and unceremonious burial attracted the rabbis' attention. Why is Rachel, the favored wife, buried along the roadside (Gen. 35:19), not even carried into nearby Bethlehem? One tradition explained that her burial place would eventually be part of the land given to the tribe of Benjamin, her son, while Bethlehem is part of Judah, given to the descendants of Leah's son. Another suggested that Jacob respects the law, as yet not given, that prohibits a man from marrying two sisters, and so determines that Rachel, whom he married second, will not be buried together with him. Yet another said that Leah prayed for Jacob but Rachel did not, so Leah, not Rachel, gained the privilege to be buried with their husband.

More often the sages tied Rachel's burial place to Jeremiah 31:15:

> A voice is heard in Ramah,
> 　lamentation and bitter weeping.
> Rachel is weeping for her children;
> 　she refuses to be comforted for her children,
> because they are no more.

Rachel was buried along the road the exiles would take when they were forced to leave Jerusalem so that she could weep for them and pray mercy on them as they passed by.

Rachel bore some blame from the midrashists i
barrenness and early death, but fared well in the tra
an intercessor for "her" children, the people of Israei.
midrash known as Lamentations Rabbah, Rachel spea
God on behalf of the people after the destruction of the tem,
and the exile to Babylon. She reminds the Sovereign of the
Universe of her love for Jacob and his for her, and her
knowledge of her father's plot to substitute her sister in
Jacob's marriage bed. Yet out of pity for her sister, Rachel
says, she helped Leah deceive Jacob, even lying under the
bed and replying to Jacob so that he would not recognize
Leah's voice.

"And if I, a creature of flesh and blood, formed of
dust and ashes, was not envious of my rival and did
not expose her to shame and contempt, why should
You, a merciful King Who lives eternally, be jealous
of idolatry in which there is no reality, and exile my
children and let them be slain by the sword?"...
Forthwith the mercy of the Holy One, Blessed be He,
was stirred, and He said, "For thy sake, Rachel, I will
restore Israel to their place." (*Lamentations Rabbah,*
Proem 24)[4]

Contemporary Midrashim

Contemporary works by Jewish authors that use the texts
and stories of Hebrew Scripture to connect the past with a
changing present often claim the designation "midrash," but
such claims become a matter of debate. Naomi Mara Hyman
reminds us that the classical midrashists worked from several
underlying assumptions:[5]

- every part of the text is written in a particular way for
  a particular purpose
- everything in the Bible is interrelated
- multiple interpretations are possible

---

[4]Cited in Barbara L. Thaw Ronson, *The Women of the Torah: Commentaries from
the Talmud, Midrash, and Kabbalah* (Northvale, N.J.: Jason Aronson, 1999), 131.

[5]Naomi Mara Hyman, *Biblical Women in the Midrash: A Sourcebook* (Northvale,
N.J.: Jason Aronson, 1997) xxviii–xxxi.

- both faith and reason are required for interpretation
- midrash is a sacred activity, bringing the divine presence into the world

Contemporary work that shares at least some of these assumptions and midrashic methods, she argues, should be designated midrash, especially when the authors' intent is to explore theological issues or to draw closer to God. Contemporary midrash on Leah and Rachel often focuses on the changing relationship between the sisters from childhood through their rivalry for Jacob's affections. The painful transformations that women's closest relationships often undergo are very much a part of modern life.

Leah's and Rachel's girlhood is typically described in the idyllic terms that often attach to childhood innocence. The girls are inseparable, taking joy in each other and the pastoral life they share. They are in every way each other's equals. In another telling, Leah is blind, and Rachel delights in being the eyes for them both.

All this abruptly stops when Jacob arrives. No longer are Leah and Rachel focused on each other. Now the attention of each is focused on Jacob, and they become each other's rivals. Jacob's clear preference for Rachel fans the flames of the sisters' envy. Yet most modern midrashim depict Rachel as devising the plot to marry Leah to Jacob first, out of love for her sister. Indeed, one version suggests that the formerly lovestruck Rachel learns something from the experience of lying under the bed, responding to Jacob's lovemaking groans, and henceforth thinks of men—her beloved Jacob included—as being rather gullible and crude. Nonetheless, Rachel gladly goes in to Jacob in her turn, and both she and Leah become Jacob's wives.

As soon as Leah's first child is conceived, some versions have it, a wedge is driven between the sisters. As Leah bears child after child and Rachel has none, their bitter feud grows. Each despises the other for receiving Jacob's attention. Rachel is deeply grieved that she has no children and devotes her attention to making herself beautiful for Jacob, hoping that each next liaison will result in pregnancy. Leah hates Rachel for primping for Jacob and fawning on him and for being Jacob's beloved. Rachel hates Leah for her fecundity, so clearly a sign of blessedness, while she herself is cursed and barren.

The modern writers differ in the depth of this rivalry and the shape it gives Jacob's family. In some versions the women exist side by side but barely acknowledge each other. Rachel is absent at Leah's births. Bilhah and Zilpah become pawns in their mistresses' rivalrous game. Their sons, and Dinah, are nearly motherless children, so consumed are Leah and Rachel by their own pain and their rivalry for Jacob's love. In other versions, each woman carries her own grief—Leah's rejection, Rachel's barrenness—but is aware of the depth of her sister's pain as well, so that although they are rivals they stop short of seeking to hurt each other further than their situation has already hurt them.

In any event, Rachel's pregnancy finally breaks the deadlock between the sisters. A thaw commences, even in the versions of the story that suggest the greatest bitterness, and Rachel and Leah are gradually able to forgive each other their previous slights. Rachel's successful delivery is cause for celebration, and her second pregnancy delights them both. Her death in childbirth, then, is a terrible blow to Leah, a second loss of her childhood companion.

Dinah in Contemporary Midrash

With Dinah, contemporary midrash focuses primarily on her voicelessness in the biblical narrative. Nearly all the modern stories of Dinah are written in the first person, in Dinah's own voice. Not all see her encounter with Shechem as a loving relationship, misunderstood by her family. Indeed, often in the contemporary midrashim Dinah is a rape survivor, and finding her voice is an important piece of her ongoing recovery from that traumatic and life-altering event. She expresses the rightful and righteous anger that she is not given an opportunity to express in the biblical narrative. She addresses her brothers, in one version, in a speech based on Jacob's own farewell words to his sons, establishing her relationship with them, and claiming her place as the twelfth of Jacob's children.

Yet the stories that give Dinah voice do not minimize her suffering. In Graetz's version, the Dinah who speaks is a fearful, cowering figure, living among her family but nearly invisible to them. She is violently assaulted by Shechem and advised by Leah that she should marry him. She resists, but cannot think of a way out. Her brothers inform her of their plan, and she objects, but cannot act to stop it. She bears a daughter, but the infant is taken from her at birth and left to die. This Dinah has a voice, it is true, but she lives as a nobody, little more than a speaking corpse.[6]

Other modern versions restore some of Dinah's dignity along with her voice. Her daughter by Shechem, Asenath, lives and marries and bears children of her own, giving Dinah comfort in her old age. She has been wronged, not only by Shechem but also by tradition, but she will no longer bear those wrongs in silence. Her voiced anger makes her, like many rape survivors today, an eloquent spokesperson for the defense of the innocent.

The Red Tent as Midrash

Is *The Red Tent* midrash? Like other contemporary works that claim the midrashic tradition, Anita Diamant's novel reflects on and develops the biblical text, giving it relevance to readers today. It is in dialogue with other works of midrash. Sometimes it follows a midrashic interpretation. On other occasions, Diamant's Dinah refers to a previous midrashic story as a tale that we, her readers, might have heard, but that we should not be so naive as to believe; she will set us right.

It is probably best not to claim that this book is midrash, but rather to highlight its midrashic elements. Diamant introduces many elements into Dinah's story that do not connect directly with the biblical text. The author is in dialogue with those interpreters through the ages who have been

---

[6]In ibid., 68–71.

fascinated by the biblical stories of Dinah and her family, stories that are full of gaps. Listening to those other interpreters, she has filled the gaps in ways that make Dinah, Leah, Rachel, and all the rest live again for a new audience. Hearing the voices with which she is in dialogue gives us a richer picture of the text itself, and of the people through the ages who have found it so fruitful for their own consideration.

QUESTIONS FOR DISCUSSION

1. How does thinking of *The Red Tent* as a midrash enhance your understanding of the novel? In what ways is the novel different from midrash?
2. Before reading *The Red Tent*, what were your impressions of Leah and Rachel? How do the midrashists' portraits of them expand your own ideas?
3. Midrash has been described as a "cognitive looking glass" that shapes the way we look at the biblical text. How has the midrash on these stories had an impact on the way you look at the biblical text?
4. In the process of filling in narrative gaps, interpreters bring much of their own experience to the interpretive task. What do you discern about what is important to the interpreters in the various midrashic interpretations?

For Further Reading

Bronner, Leila Leah. *From Eve to Esther: Rabbinic Reconstructions of Biblical Women*. Louisville: Westminster John Knox Press, 1994.

Hyman, Naomi Mara. *Biblical Women in the Midrash: A Sourcebook*. Northvale, N.J.: Jason Aronson, 1997.

Neusner, Jacob. *Genesis Rabbah: The Judaic Commentary to the Book of Genesis: A New American Translation*. 3 vol. Atlanta: Scholars Press, 1985.

———. *Invitation to Midrash: The Workings of Rabbinic Bible Interpretation*. Atlanta: Scholars Press, 1998.

CHAPTER 4

Where Is God in All This?

Goddesses and the Emergence of Yahwism

> When I was old enough to ask what it was like on the
> day that my father arrived, she said that the presence of El
> hovered over him, which is why he was worthy of notice.
> Zilpah told me that El was the god of thunder, high places,
> and awful sacrifice. El could demand that a father cut off his
> son—cast him out into the desert, or slaughter him outright.
> This was a hard, strange god, alien and cold, but, she
> conceded, a consort powerful enough for the Queen of
> Heaven, whom she loved in every shape and name.
>
> (*Red Tent*, 13)

> Now the LORD said to Abram, "Go from your country
> and your kindred and your father's house to the land that I
> will show you. I will make of you a great nation, and I will
> bless you, and make your name great, so that you will be a
> blessing. I will bless those who bless you, and the one who
> curses you I will curse; and in you all the families of the
> earth shall be blessed."
>
> (Gen. 12:1–3)

The Hebrew Bible, even the stories of Genesis, is written from the standpoint of the developed monotheism of its authors and compilers, not the more fluid religious perspective of its subjects. As readers of the English Bible, we encounter one God, first as Creator, then as sole Divine Sovereign. This God is called simply "God" (Hebrew *'el* or *'elohim*) or by the title "Lord" (Hebrew *'adonai*) or by the personal name YHWH (usually translated LORD in caps and small caps). Other gods (note the lowercase) have names, are represented by idols, and are worshiped by other people, but the Bible's main subjects, those who will become (by the end of Genesis) the people of Israel, worship (or are expected to worship) the one, true, invisible God alone.

Thus one of the most surprising aspects of *The Red Tent*, particularly for many of its Christian readers, is the variety of deities the characters in its pages honor. Diamant transports us to a time before monotheism, and we hear the name of Abram's god, El, alongside many others. Even the Bible recognizes that Israel's forefathers worshiped other gods (Josh. 24:2). In *The Red Tent* gods and goddesses in almost dizzying variety are invoked as the creators, sustainers, and destroyers of human life. Human beings honor them with varying degrees of loyalty. Worship practices are in many ways very different from those with which we are familiar. Temples and religious professionals exist, but most of the rituals that Dinah's family practice seem to be carried out at home, by family members.

Many Gods, Many Stories

The light was beginning to fade when Jacob and Esau began to tell stories. Our bondswomen brought lamps and Esau's slaves kept them filled with oil, so the light from the flames danced upon the faces of my family, suddenly grown numerous. Tabea and I sat knee to knee, listening to the story of our great-grandfather Abram, who had left the ancient home in Ur where the moon was worshiped in the name of Ninna and

Ningal, and gone to Haran where the voice of El had come to him and directed him to Canaan. In the south, Abram had done great deeds—killing a thousand men with a single blow because El-Abram had given him the power of ten thousand. (*Red Tent*, 136)

When ancient humans told their stories, they also told the stories of their gods, who represented the power felt in the universe. Individuals saw themselves as particularly related to certain gods. An important ancestor would be connected in the family lore with the god who was seen to have chosen or particularly aided him or her, and the god would have special status in the family, honored in succeeding generations. Cities, too, had deities who were their special patrons, and a city would appeal to its god or goddess for success in war or delivery from famine.

Like humans, the gods were understood to be related to one another in extended families and to have spheres of responsibility like administrators in local governments or overseers of large estates. These familial and administrative roles typically were communicated in the form of myths, stories that could easily be remembered and repeated and that described the deities' characteristics and relationships.

Just as in extended human families, gods and goddesses related to one another, and human beings related to them both. The fact of goddess-worship is not evidence of a separatist women's religious practice. Both men and women worshiped goddesses as well as gods, and for many of the same reasons: protection, health and healing, economic survival and prosperity, the provision of offspring.

Yet neither should we imagine a sort of ancient gender neutrality in the imaging of deity. Reality and power were structured according to gender, and goddesses' roles were those that befit these structures of society. Goddesses defined "femaleness" in family, culture, and society. Their behavior modeled (sometimes negatively) how human women were expected to behave. Goddesses represented the whole range of female roles: sister, wife, mother, mother-in-law, daughter, lover, provider, nurse, teacher, counselor, producer of goods necessary to life. Goddesses were capable of love, loyalty, nurture, and companionship, as well as jealousy, rage, manipulation, and murder. In all these ways they reflected the "female" in ancient society.

The Sumero-Akkadian Pantheon

Mesopotamian life and religious practices may be traced to the ancient region of Sumer in southern Mesopotamia, where in many ways modern civilization began around 3000 B.C.E. Major Sumerian cities included Nippur, Adab, Lagash, Umma, Larsa, Erech, Ur, and Eridu. Abram was born in Ur (compare Gen. 11:28, 31; 15:7; 1 Chr. 11:35; Neh. 9:7). The Sumerians evidently invented cuneiform writing, later taken up by the Babylonians and Assyrians. Sumerians and their descendants in Mesopotamia and the surrounding regions worshiped gods who can be described according to their family relationships, although the various roles can be difficult to make clear. The following details about these gods may enhance your understanding of Diamant's references. The primeval parents, the originating gods, were the male An, representing the heavens, and the female Ki, representing the earth. Ki only appears in this primeval myth, however. Ki's role as ruler of earth is taken over by her son, Enlil. Enki is said to be the younger brother of Enlil, but his mother is usually depicted as Nammu, goddess of the watery depths. The goddesses Ninlil and Ninhursag are sisters of Enlil and Enki and share the role of the mother goddess. Ninhursag is usually understood as goddess of wildlife and the power of the ground and as the sexual partner of Enki. Ninlil is understood to be Enlil's consort. Enlil and Ninlil are the parents of the moon god and goddess, Nanna and Ningal, whose children, in turn, are the sun god Utu and his sister Inanna.

Enki, associated with the waters as his mother was, is described in a myth in which he and the goddess Ninmah, shaper of newborns, argued about their importance to humans. Ninmah claimed that she held human destiny by shaping the newborn, while Enki argued that his power over society was the more important role. Ninmah proceeded to create defective humans—palsied, blind, deaf, and the like— but Enki was able to find each of them a place in society. When Enki's turn to create came, however, the figure he was able to fashion without the help of a mother-goddess was so deformed that Ninmah could not assign it any societal role. Ninmah accepted defeat, but at this very point Enki acknowledged the indispensability of the goddess in forming human beings. The myth, in which Enki is ultimately seen to gain in power at Ninmah's expense, both emphasizes and narrows the female role by associating it with procreative power.

Nanshe, goddess of fish and fowl, is a daughter of Enki, and is associated both with dream interpretation and social justice. Uttu, goddess of weaving, is also Enki's daughter, through an unusual set of circumstances. Enki's sexual relations with Ninhursag produced Ninnisiga; with Ninnisiga, Enki fathered Ninkurra; with Ninkurra, Enki fathered Ninimma; with Ninimma, Enki fathered Uttu. When Uttu grew up, however, Ninhursag insisted that Uttu first require gifts of Enki before she allowed him to sleep with her. With these gifts, Uttu represents the properly married woman. Interestingly, Uttu, the "domestic" goddess and the first real wife, was the first of Enki's sexual partners to have difficulty in pregnancy and childbirth.

To Uttu and other goddesses fell the responsibilities of what might be termed the arts of survival: the transformation of natural materials into clothing, food, and drink. Uttu, to whom Bilhah is loyal in *The Red Tent*, was honored as the goddess who brought to human women the transformation of wool into clothing and blankets so that "their babies, swaddled in wool blankets, no longer died of the cold but grew up to offer up sacrifice to the gods" (*Red Tent*, 80). Leah particularly honors Ninkasi, who transformed barley into beer. Nisba, goddess of grain, was the provider of bread. Along with these three was often grouped Ninurra, goddess of pottery. Without these womanly pursuits, understood to be given by the goddesses, civilization at its most basic level could not exist.

Perhaps because the everyday practices of brewing, weaving, and the like represented some of the highest technological achievements of society, goddesses were also seen as the keepers of wisdom and learning, and "higher" cultural pursuits such as song and dreams (e.g., Zilpah's

Nanshe). Incidentally, this rarely translated into high levels of education for human women. With the exception of Enheduanna, daughter of the Sumerian king Sargon and high priestess of the moon-god Nanna, who wrote beautiful lyric poetry in honor of Inanna, women were rarely literate. The society assumed they needed no education other than what they received from their mothers.

Arguably the most mysterious and frightening power associated with goddesses was that of health and healing, and specifically of childbirth. Gula, the healer and Rachel's special deity, holds not only the power of the womb but also the lore of herbs and balms. Incantations in childbirth were spoken to her, and the song of the fearless mother refers to her:

Fear not, the time is coming
Fear not, your bones are strong
Fear not, help is nearby
Fear not, Gula is near… (*Red Tent*, 176)

The skillful midwife was understood to be blessed by Gula. Gula was not all-powerful in the birth chamber. In particular, the goddess-become-human Lamastu was seen as the killer of babies. She was the sister of Inanna and, as such, a high-ranking goddess. Expelled from heaven, she became a particularly powerful evil spirit. In the ancient tales, Lamastu sometimes posed as a midwife, then strangled or poisoned the infant. She is often imaged with a dog's head and may in this guise be related to the dog-shaped death deity of which Dinah speaks, though Dinah images this divine figure as male. Amulets for the mother and the newborn, and incantations banishing Lamastu, were used to ward off her deadly presence.

INANNA

Inanna (or in Diamant's spelling, Innana), also called Ishtar, functioned in the Sumerian pantheon as the nondomesticated woman—the powerful, dangerous, desirable female far from the life of the typical human woman. She represented sexual joy and procreative power, not dutiful wifehood. Jacob calls Leah "Innana" during their wedding week together, when they have no task in the world but to fulfill one another. Although some epic stories involve Inanna's children, she is not depicted in the role of a proper mother. She remains something of an anomaly, uncontrollable and dangerous, perhaps threatening to the order of society, yet expressing life's vital energy.

Despite her seductive power, Inanna was portrayed in myth as the proper maiden, resisting the urging of her suitor Dumuzi that she tell lies to her mother so that she could tarry with him in the moonlight. Delighted when Dumuzi asked properly for her hand in marriage, she eagerly prepared for the wedding, adorning herself with makeup and jewelry and making sure that Dumuzi provided sufficient food for the wedding feast. Their marriage was splendidly celebrated.

Yet Inanna, in the ancient tales, neither spun nor wove, the primary tasks of every ordinary woman (and generally depicted as the pastimes of goddesses as well). She had power and authority, but its sphere was not clearly defined. She was depicted as restless and wandering about. One of her roles was as goddess of the morning and evening stars, those points of heavenly light that seemed to wander among the more properly fixed constellations. Inanna represented the boundaries of gender and gender roles, but by breaking the norms, her social function was, paradoxically, to reinforce those norms.

Readers of *The Red Tent* are well aware that Dinah and the other women of her family give Innana a far larger role than that described here, associating her with the Great Mother, Queen of Heaven, and patron of the rain, as well as the giver of pleasure. This is not necessarily historical inaccuracy on Diamant's part. Ancient religious practice showed great fluidity, and the name and characteristics attributed to one god in a certain time and place could be merged with another, or even several others, elsewhere and at another time. Indeed, one of the significant challenges for developing monotheism was to curb this tendency to see the gods as essentially nearly interchangeable. In this novel Jacob represents the early stages of monotheism, but still tolerates his wives' worship of Innana to the extent that he is able to imagine her as an extension of El. Jacob becomes uneasy when Innana connects with other Mesopotamian deities whose worship Jacob understands to be antithetical to devotion to El.

The Place of El

The *Red Tent* pantheon is fluid. Alongside the Sumero-Akkadian deities we also hear of gods whose names were originally Ugaritic or Canaanite: the father-god El, his consort Asherah, and their offspring Yam, Mot, and the war-goddess Anat, who entered into sexual union with the storm-god Baal. El is represented in *The Red Tent* as the god of Abram, Isaac, and Jacob, the one who demanded that Abram be willing to sacrifice his son and in obedience to whom Jacob circumcises his infant sons and the other males of his clan. As readers familiar with the Hebrew Bible, we recognize here the god that the Bible proclaims as the one God, creator of heaven and earth, due exclusive worship and honor.

In Diamant's retelling El is not the only god, and even those (such as Jacob) who typically honor him alone sometimes turn to other deities for assistance in extremity. Yet in this version El is a powerful god, and the women of Jacob's family honor Asherah, whom they also call the Queen of Heaven, showing that they recognize El and his consort as the family deities.

In the biblical record, some of the oldest traditions depict Yahweh (the personal name of Israel's God revealed to Moses) as equivalent with El and enthroned over an assembly of other gods (Ps. 82; 1 Kings 22:19). The exclusive monotheism that later characterized Israelite religion did not completely annihilate these earlier references. One tradition behind the Pentateuch (Genesis—Deuteronomy) explicitly identifies Yahweh with El, depicting the patriarchs as worshiping a god they knew as El, who made himself known as Yahweh only later, to Moses.

Early Yahwism may well have identified Asherah or the Queen of Heaven as the consort of El/Yahweh. If so, female members of the Yahwist communities in particular likely would have honored her, just as Dinah, her mothers, and the other women associated with Isaac and Jacob do. As the mother goddess, she would have been worshiped as the giver of fertility and a protector of women and children. It is harder to say whether she would have been widely associated with Inanna, though the fluidity in local worship practice would certainly make it possible. Indeed, this shadowy identity of the Queen of Heaven—whether she is the mother-goddess associated with El, or the untamed goddess of pleasure associated with Inanna—could explain both the attribution of motherly characteristics to Innana in Diamant's retelling and the uneasiness expressed by male members of the El-clan toward the women's practices in the red tent.

The general decline of importance of goddesses in ancient religion coincided with the rise of more complicated political structures such as nation-states. Civilization was gradually defined less as the technologies that provided for humanity's basic needs—the products of women's work and the domain of goddesses—and more as the political alliances and military conquests that were the domain of males and ruled over by gods. Order and stability, established by political structures, became a more important cultural value than the cycle of life and fertility represented primarily by the goddesses. Goddesses continued to receive loyalty, particularly from female members of society, but their relationship to a male deity as wife, sister, or daughter increasingly defined their role.

In later Israelite religion, El/Yahweh gradually absorbed the roles of the other gods and goddesses. Yahweh, not a mother goddess, is creator of the earth and all that is in it (Gen. 1; Isa. 45:5–7). Yahweh is said explicitly to control the rain, and thereby the fertility of the land, taking over the role of the storm-god Baal (Pss. 29; 147:8–9). Baal becomes the rival of Yahweh rather than his relative, an (inappropriate) alternative for the loyalty of the people (1 Kings 18). Yahweh, according to the biblical record, is the one who opens and closes the womb, giving him dominion over even that most "feminine" of goddess-roles, human reproduction (Gen. 29:31; 1 Sam. 1:5–6; Isa. 66:9). The Bible also preserves some female imagery for Yahweh, perhaps an attempt to dispel the need for female deities by recognizing in one God both male and female characteristics (e.g., Isa. 66:13). Once Yahweh was understood to provide everything that the people needed, other gods became extraneous and seen as a threat to Yahweh's dominance. Monotheism had become a reality for Israel.

But this monotheistic state of affairs is long after the period of the patriarchs. It is quite reasonable to imagine that people in Middle Bronze Age Canaan would have worshiped both El and his Asherah. The women, in particular, would have offered obeisance to the Queen of Heaven, whom they might have also associated with Inanna, as a combination of their mothers' religion and the family El cult.

Egyptian Gods and Goddesses

When Dinah moves to Egypt, she encounters new deities: Osiris, Isis, Bes, Set, Tawaret. Like the Mesopotamian and Canaanite gods, these deities are related to one another in complicated extended family relationships and have responsibilities for particular areas of human life. The complicated saga of Isis and Osiris is likely the most widely known of the Egyptian myths. Isis was widowed when her brother-husband Osiris was thrown into the Nile by another brother, Typhon. She wandered the world until she located the body of Osiris. Along the way, Isis adopted a son who was Osiris's child by another sister. She found and mourned over Osiris's body, but Typhon stole it yet again, dismembered it, and distributed the pieces all over Egypt. Isis, still faithful, continued to search until she reassembled Osiris's body and briefly reanimated him. The child who was subsequently born to them, though, emerged from the womb early and had weak legs. Isis's story summarizes the experiences and socially expected roles of many women: sisterhood, marriage, and widowhood; care for children, the sick, and the dead; love, betrayal, and bereavement; loyalty and unswerving devotion. She was Egypt's primary mother-goddess, though Tawaret also aided laboring mothers, and Bes protected infant children.

Representations of the Deities

Many of the gods Dinah describes have shapes she recognizes in pottery or stone figures: the statue of Tawaret she encounters early in her stay in Egypt, the pitcher that Benia brings her from the market in the shape of the goddess. Dinah speaks of Anubis, the god of death, as having the shape of a dog. The breaking of Dinah's hymen in her coming-of-age ceremony is accomplished with a small statue in the shape of a grinning frog. Rachel steals Laban's teraphim, the representations of his household gods. All the women recognize that this loss will infuriate Laban. Only the discovery that Rachel has defiled them with her menstrual blood dissuades Laban from demanding their return.

It is clear from the way the characters in *The Red Tent* speak of and behave toward the deities that they do not simplistically equate the gods and goddesses with the figures of clay or stone. But it is equally clear that the figures are more than mere statues. They are ritual objects that participate in the power of the gods they represent. Possession of them is important, and their loss is distressing—for Laban, first by theft and then by what he considers irreparable defilement, and for the women, when Jacob discovers the images' presence and destroys them. The loss of the last of these is so distressing to Zilpah that Dinah connects the event with her death.

The Importance of Worship Place

The small size of some representations of the deities, such that Rachel can sweep them into her skirts and carry them in a bundle on her back, does not mean that worship practices are necessarily so portable. Some representations of the deities cannot easily be carried. Asherah lends her name to the figure asherah, or sacred pole, that can be purchased and set up (Laban buys one for his daughters), but once in place is generally considered to be a permanent fixture, sacralizing the place where it is erected.

When Jacob and his family plan to leave Laban, a major concern for the women is the fact that they will leave the places where their gods abide. Zilpah in particular is distressed by the prospect of leaving. "'I cannot go,' she burst out. 'I cannot leave the holy tree, which is the source of my power. Or the bamah, which is soaked in my offerings. How will the gods know where I am if I am not here to serve them? Who will protect me? Sisters, we will be beset by demons'" (*Red Tent*, 88). Bilhah assures her that every place has holy places, and Rachel witnesses that even the names of the gods have remarkable power, even as she schemes to take the teraphim.

The Sacred Grove at Mamre

Diamant creates one significant holy place in the pages of *The Red Tent*: a sacred grove at Mamre, where Rebecca functions as an oracle. Dinah's perception of Mamre is strongly shaped by her impressions of "the Grandmother" and her ill-fated hopes of impressing her. Yet enough details emerge for the reader to get a sense of how a deity might have been honored in a sacred place such as this, with an oracle as religious functionary.

Rebecca reigns at Mamre as a high priestess, with acolytes to attend to her needs and the offerings of pilgrims and gifts of family to sustain her. Rituals of song, dance, and sacrifice accompany the various annual festivals. The attendants at Mamre also observe the rituals and libations at the new moon that Dinah's mothers observe at their own red tent. Rebecca welcomes all pilgrims who come to her and provides, as appropriate, healing or easing of pain, blessings or warnings, or auguries of the future. She refers to her sacred grove as "the navel of the world" (153), and regards her life there as service to the Queen of Heaven.

Rebecca also enforces the rituals she considers essential to worship of the goddess, in particular the ritual for a young woman's coming of age. When she discovers that Dinah's cousin Tabea has reached womanhood without the appropriate rites, she flies into a rage and curses her mother, then banishes both mother and daughter from her sacred tent. Dinah is deeply distressed, but Leah explains:

"It was not her intention to harm Tabea. I think she loved her well enough, but she had no choice. She was defending her mother and herself, me and your aunties, you and your daughters after you. She was defending the ways of our mothers and their mothers, and the great mother, who goes by many names, but who is in danger of being forgotten." (*Red Tent*, 157)

Because the rituals and the knowledge are in danger of being forgotten, Leah explains, Rebecca enforces the rituals and punishes those who do not observe them. No less than blessing and foretelling, this is a function of her religious role as oracle of Mamre.

Honoring the Gods

Religious functionaries such as Rebecca encourage proper performance of the rituals and denounce those who neglect them, but they cannot oversee their practice. It is up to ordinary people, men like Jacob and women like Dinah and her mothers, to honor the deities by the appropriate performance of religious acts. Jacob's family, who live in relative rural isolation, demonstrate particularly well this lack of reliance on religious professionals. Jacob circumcises his own sons. The women perform their own rituals to welcome the new moon and to honor the gods who give food, wine, and beer. As they prepare to cross the river, Jacob and his wives pour a libation into its waters. Comings of age, marriages, and burials all take place in the family.

The Sacred in the Routine

For ancient people settled enough to practice agriculture, annual festivals typically marked significant times in the agricultural year. They celebrated festivals at the beginnings or endings of important harvests, or when the rains returned to the land after seasons of little or no precipitation. Typically these celebrations revolved around food, eaten in greater quantity and variety than would have been featured in the typical diet. Meat was rarely if ever eaten except at celebratory events. Those whose daily lives were more settled might travel to a central location to celebrate a festival: Jacob's and Esau's families meet at the grove at Mamre to mark the barley harvest. In such gatherings the celebration was typically more elaborate, with music, dancing, and storytelling accompanying the feasts.

The nature of women's bodies and women's work meant that they were the ones who performed many of the everyday or frequent religious rituals. Women's acts of transformation—particularly of grain into bread and barley into beer—were marked by small rites of honor to the goddesses of these processes. In Dinah's family, the women celebrate the arrival of each new moon, emerging from the red tent to sing and dance. In Egypt, Dinah honors Isis daily as a way of thanking the gods of Egypt, whose stories she does not know, for giving her her son. She makes weekly offerings to the Queen of Heaven by feeding a bit of bread to the ducks in the garden. Different ancient peoples had slightly different rituals, but most were similar to these: small symbols, bows or kisses, daily prayers, or tiny sacrifices, reminding common people that their lives depended on the favor of the gods and that they owed honor to the divine.

Life Passages

Many people today who are content to spend Sunday sleeping late and reading the newspaper nonetheless seek out religious functionaries at significant life passages. Christenings or baptisms, marriages, and funerals often bring people inside the walls of the church, or face-to-face with a minister. The individuals who participate in such services may or may not experience a personal connection with the divine, but often they are fulfilling some deep sense that this is the right thing to do, beyond issues of social propriety or what family members expect of them.

Concerning the ancient world, too, it is impossible to say with certainty to what extent the participants in religious rituals understood themselves to be connected with the divine. The gods, particularly chief gods, were sometimes imagined as either distant or capricious, so ordinary humans may have performed their ritual acts without a strong sense that the gods were affected by what they did. Even so, the general sense of the immanence of deity, that the gods were in some sense involved in every aspect of human life, meant that ancient people were more likely than most moderns to consider their acts of worship a small piece of the great drama that kept the cosmos in proper functioning.

The religious nature of life rituals, though, does not mean that ancient peoples always sought out the services of a religious professional such as a priest, or went to a temple or sanctuary of the gods. For many this was simply not possible. In the absence of religious professionals, certain individuals in the family presided over religious ceremonies. As we have seen, sacred places could be where a family lived, at a particular tree, on top of a hill, or wherever an asherah was set up. Rituals were performed within the family and passed on from generation to generation.

Marriage

In the ancient world, the primary rituals involved with marriage were social and economic ones, representing the transfer of a bride from one family to another and the accompanying transfers of money or gifts that signified both families' acceptance of the match. These gifts, as dowry or bride-price or both, were sometimes quite large. The prestige of the families and the commitment they were able to make to the new household were matters of honor.

The marriage ceremony itself varied greatly, depending on local custom and economic status. It could be rather simple, as Leah's and Rachel's were, or quite elaborate, involving days of feasting and complicated ceremonies moving the woman from one household to another. In any case the blessings of the gods would be invoked on the couple, and often they would spend an extended time alone together in a bridal tent or chamber. In the case of a concubine or slave-wife, there might be no formal ceremony whatsoever. Sexual union would be understood to establish the relationship (the fact of sexual activity did not by itself signify marriage; a man could, and often did, have sex with female slaves without changing their status in any way). Second marriages (for the bride) also typically entailed little ceremony, since a woman was not changing status from virgin to wife. In general, although a wedding in ancient times could be a festive (and often an expensive!) ceremony, its specifically religious significance was less than for other important life events.

CHILDBIRTH

As *The Red Tent* makes clear, childbirth was the greatest threat to the life of a woman who survived her own childhood. Women could be in labor for days with a difficult birth. Often a midwife could do little to correct a breech or face presentation. Postpartum infection sometimes took the life of mothers who survived labor and delivery. No wonder childbirth was a religious occasion as well as a physical trial for a woman. To bring new life into the world, a woman had to pass close to the gates of death.

Dinah mentions the presence of a priest at some births, and religious professionals were sometimes called to attend the birthing mother, to keep away demons and draw the attention of benevolent deities. But often the midwife was expected to be the religious professional as well. Her stock-in-trade included not only blocks for the laboring mother to squat on, reeds for removing blood and mucus, and string for tying off the umbilical cord, but also herbs and balms, many of which were understood to have magical properties, and incantations.

Dinah speaks with distaste of the kinds of medicinal preparations she finds used in Egypt, based on dung and urine and dried animal parts. Such concoctions were used, despite their unpleasantness, for their supposed magical effects, attracting the strength or other desired quality of the animal from which they came, or repelling an evil spirit imaged as the animal's enemy.

Dinah's reputation in Egypt grows when she sings the song of the strong mother or lashes out in anger at an unfeeling father in her own tongue. These expressions, whose words are not understood by the people around her, are assumed to be incantations, and they function the way incantations often do. The mood and tone, rather than the words, make an impression on those who hear, and they assume that the gods are appeased or summoned to judgment by what is said. But the midwife's use of incantation was not limited to foreign words misunderstood by those around her. Like countless midwives of ancient times, Dinah, Rachel, Inna, and Meryt speak incantations and prayers as part of their regular work, to invite the protective deities and fend off the demons, to strengthen the fainting spirits of the laboring mothers and calm the fears of the attending women. These ancient midwives were the priestesses as well as the physicians in the mortally dangerous time of childbirth, when women in labor needed every aid that religion—or magic or medicine—could afford them.

CIRCUMCISION

As Dinah's observations show us, the Israelites were not the only ancient people who practiced circumcision, though the practice was by no means universal. For other ancient cultures the removal of the foreskin of the penis was often a male marriage or coming-of-age rite, performed on young men (as Dinah's son Re-mose exemplifies). Israelites were in many cultural circles known as distinctive—and sometimes regarded as barbaric—for circumcising male infants.

Whenever circumcision was performed, it was a fairly simple surgical procedure, with a relatively low risk of infection or other complications. Nonetheless, it was not performed routinely or for health purposes. It was a religious rite whenever it was done, connecting this male with other males in his religious community, and identifying him to the community's gods. When a priest was available, he was often trained and skilled in the procedure, but among Israelites the father often circumcised his own sons. Naturally this involved some pain, particularly for those men who were circumcised past infancy, but healing generally took only a few days. As in the case of Re-mose, this enforced leisure could be the occasion of feasting and other family or community celebrations held to mark the entrance of a boy into manhood.

Circumcision permanently marked the circumcised man as different from uncircumcised men in surrounding areas.

Circumcision reminded a man regularly that he was different from "outsiders," part of a distinct community that typically had high boundary markers, often including the worship of particular gods. Indeed, the Shechemites' willingness to be circumcised may imply a certain willingness to enter Jacob's community and honor Jacob's god, though the biblical text does not explicitly say so. If so, the acts of Simeon and Levi are an even greater betrayal of their father. When Re-mose goes uncircumcised as an infant, Dinah realizes with some pain that her father's god will not recognize him. At the same time, she is fiercely glad that her son will not bear a mark that recalls his own father's betrayal and murder.

FIRST MENSES

While *The Red Tent* tells us relatively little about male coming-of-age ceremonies, it describes in detail the rituals that Dinah's mother and the other women in her family enact when she menstruates for the first time. They bring her into the red tent, give her fortified wine, paint her with henna, anoint her with perfume, and feed her delicacies.

> In the next moment, I found myself outside with my mother and my aunts. We were in the wheat patch in the heart of the garden—a hidden place where grain dedicated to sacrifice was grown. The soil had been tilled in preparation for planting after the moon's return, and I was naked, lying facedown on the cool soil. I shivered. My mother put my cheek to the ground and loosened my hair around me. She arranged my arms wide, "to embrace the earth," she whispered. She bent my knees and pulled the soles of my feet together until they touched, "to give the first blood back to the land," said Leah. I could feel the night air on my sex, and it was strange and wonderful to be so open under the sky.
>
> My mothers gathered around: Leah above me, Bilhah at my left hand, Zilpah's hand on the back of my legs. I was grinning like the frog, half asleep, in love with them all. Rachel's voice behind me broke the silence. "Mother! Innana! Queen of the Night!

> Accept the blood offering of your daughter, in her mother's name, in your name. In her blood may she live, in her blood may she give life."
>
> It did not hurt. The oil eased the entry, and the narrow triangle fit perfectly as it entered me. I faced the west while the little goddess faced east as she broke the lock on my womb. When I cried out, it was not so much pain but surprise and perhaps even pleasure, for it seemed to me that the Queen herself was lying on top of me, with Dumuzi her consort beneath me. I was like a slip of cloth, caught between their lovemaking, warmed by the great passion. (*Red Tent*, 172–73)

Dinah's mothers identify with the belief, widely held in antiquity, that a young woman's hymen should be ritually broken in a ceremony involving women only. The blood, along with her first menstrual blood, should be carefully returned to the earth. These practices tended to correlate with a belief in a powerful Mother-Goddess, responsible for the fertility of human beings and of the earth itself. As we also see in *The Red Tent*, in Dinah's time such practices were already beginning to be set aside in favor of practices that gave the new husband the right to break his bride's hymen, and made the blood-stained bridal sheet a token of her virgin status. This corresponded to a shift away from the emphasis on cycle and fertility associated with the mother-goddess and toward an emphasis on order and status (the husband's family could observe the proof that the bride was a "proper" candidate for marriage), values generally associated more closely with male deities.

DEATH AND BURIAL

Ancient societies differed on the particular nature of the afterlife and the place of the dead. Death was often imaged as a kind of rebirth, and corpses were buried crouched in a fetal position, awaiting birth again beyond the grave. Across many cultures, women often readied the body for burial and performed rituals of preparation—perhaps because women were often the ones who tended to the needs of the physical body, including the sick and dying, or perhaps because they represented maternal nurture once again as the soul awaited rebirth.

Dinah describes burials in Mesopotamia and in Egypt. In both instances the dead loved one is adorned with jewelry and shrouded as richly as possible. The corpse is placed in a fetal position and buried in a place of honor, the women leading the keening, a shrill cry of lament that signaled to all around that the family was in mourning. In the Hebrew Bible, women lead death laments as well (Jer. 9:17–18).

Conclusion

Diamant draws together several strands of ancient myth and practice to imagine what religious life might have been like for Dinah's family and others whom she encounters. As the novel makes clear, ancient peoples assumed that they lived in a world populated with divine beings. Gods and goddesses abounded, and humans could cultivate their assistance by any number of acts of devotion, or incur their wrath by careless omissions. The well-being of individuals, families, and cities depended on divine favor. Women particularly were aware of the involvement of the gods in their daily lives, and especially in the conditions surrounding pregnancy and childbirth. During the Middle Bronze Age, powerful goddesses provided both daily necessities and aid in childbearing, and women especially honored these goddesses with their devotion.

QUESTIONS FOR DISCUSSION

---

1. How do the myths about the various gods and goddesses shape your perception of them? Do the myths make it difficult for you to think of these characters as deities, or do they invite you to imagine how the gods and goddesses might relate to human beings?

2. Consider the various roles that are often attributed to Mary, mother of Jesus, in Christian communities: Queen of Heaven, intercessor, ideal mother. How are these roles,

and the practices associated with them, similar to and different from the ways Dinah and her female family members relate to Innana?

3. What everyday religious rituals do you practice? How might greater emphasis on ritual give you a stronger sense of connection to the Divine in your daily life?

4. What is the significance of rituals practiced in your religious community or communities? How does your community incorporate new practices, or discontinue practices that are no longer meaningful?

For Further Reading

Frymer-Kensky, Tikva. *In the Wake of the Goddesses: Women, Culture, and the Biblical Transformation of a Pagan Myth.* New York: The Free Press, 1992.

Ruether, Rosemary Radford. *Goddesses and the Divine Feminine: A Western Religious History.* Berkeley: University of California Press, 2005.

CHAPTER 5

Families, Natural and Invented

"I will call you daughter in front of my brother and his wife," she said. "I will tell them that you served in my household and that my son took you, a virgin, with my consent. I will say that you helped me to escape from the barbarians. You will become my daughter-in-law, and I will be your mistress. You will bear your son on my knees, and he will be a prince of Egypt."

(*Red Tent*, 215)

I have become a stranger to my kindred, an alien to my mother's children.

(Ps.69:8)

The Red Tent is a deliciously rich tale of family relationships. Many of the details of these relationships are foreign to us. How many of us could imagine bearing and raising an infant, knowing all along that someone else has legal claim to the child, and teaching your baby to call that other woman "Mother"? And who among us would think of four sisters as our mothers, not only because of the way they relate to us (this happens sometimes in large extended families) but also because they all share the bed of the man we know as Father? Such exotic scenarios transport us to a different time and place and invite us to imagine situations we would never come across in real life.

And yet these characters experience emotions that are familiar to us: love and passion, pain and loss, solidarity and betrayal. In these strange sagas we relive our own stories. Exploring the web of familial relationships in which Dinah finds herself at various stages of her life helps us think through how her experiences are ours as well.

A Daughter of Four Mothers

Undoubtedly the richest emotional ties in *The Red Tent* are those of Dinah to her mother, Leah, and her aunts, Rachel, Zilpah, and Bilhah. Dinah explains that she received from each of her mothers, as she often calls them, different gifts: "Leah gave me birth and her splendid arrogance. Rachel showed me where to place the midwife's bricks and how to fix my hair. Zilpah made me think. Bilhah listened" (*Red Tent*, 2). In addition, as the only daughter in the family, Dinah is often treated more as another of her mothers' sisters than as their child. She is present in the red tent as a nursing infant and again as a nubile young woman, but also in the time in between, the childhood that she remembers so vividly. During this childhood, she hears her mothers' stories again and again, learns to repeat them, memorizes every detail. She observes her mother and her aunts, discovers the unique characteristics of each woman, and learns how to see the world through their eyes.

Dinah learns her mothers' skills as well. While she is never as accomplished in cooking as Leah, she carefully observes and learns from Rachel the skills of midwifery and the knowledge of herbs, and eventually becomes Rachel's apprentice. Every woman must be capable of spinning, and so Leah dutifully teaches her daughter. When Dinah proves unskillful, Leah becomes exasperated with her and strikes her. Humiliated and in tears, Dinah seeks out Bilhah, who not only trains Dinah's hands to the spindle but also teaches her the ancient stories about the origin of spinning thread and weaving cloth.

Children today, especially daughters, also learn their mothers' skills. Often a mother can prepare a meal more quickly without her children's help than with it, but she plans to take extra time when possible so that she can pass along whatever culinary knowledge she possesses. Some little girls will beg scraps of cloth from mother's sewing to dress their dolls or, when a little older, will insist on needle and thread to make real doll garments. Or in today's world, a daughter is as likely to learn how to read the stock market reports and invest her own money, or write her own books, in imitation of her mother's work.

Some of the most significant moments within the red tent occur in the rituals that the women enact together when one of them marks a momentous life event. Leah's first delivery is frightening to all the women, who have never seen childbirth before, but after she bears a son safely, they enact the ritual of burying the placenta and proceed to pamper mother and son for the first month of the baby's life.

Dinah describes the onset of her menses as another such expression of the community of women, whose membership she has just properly entered. The rather elaborate rituals are launched smoothly, almost effortlessly, as if the entire family of women had been waiting for just this moment. In a sense they had. Because Dinah is the sole daughter and it was clear that she was nearing womanhood, her mother and her aunts likely made some necessary preparations unbeknownst to her. But in another sense, these rituals need no preparation. They are an expression of who these women are and the community they create.

Death is accompanied by rituals that fulfill both physical and emotional needs. Death, whether of the aged or of stillborn infants, is followed in its turn by life, and the women mark each progression with rituals of physical care, song, and spoken (or whispered) word.

While the various rituals the women perform have religious significance, as we have already seen, their primary significance to the story Dinah relates is the community of women they bring into being and sustain. When Dinah becomes a wife without a wedding and even more when she leaves her family behind, it is the loss of this sisterhood of women that we grieve with her as much as her physical separation from the familiar surroundings of her childhood.

In our day, large or extended families are more likely to have formal rituals than small nuclear families. Pick up any women's magazine around the holidays, though, and you are likely to find suggestions for creating and sustaining family rituals, even for a family of two or three. Human beings, it seems, are hungry for rituals that bind us together in community, and particularly the community of parents and children.

Dinah is so much a combination of all her mothers, and her life is such an expression of their community, that it may be surprising to read her offhand comments about the tensions between them, and especially between Leah and Rachel. At these moments we recognize that Dinah is torn between two people deeply beloved to her. How often is she pressed into the role of communicating essential information that Leah and Rachel prefer not to address to each other directly? How often does one sister attempt to play Dinah off against the other, and how does Dinah, especially as a young child, negotiate such a difficult role? Does she ever resent being put in such a place and devise her own strategies for exacting retaliation? Answers to these questions are not part of the story Dinah tells her readers. Still, we can understand this kind of triangulation, and we sympathize with Dinah's position. It is not always easy to live in a family, and adults do, unfortunately, create alliances with children for their own purposes. Dinah's honesty about the pervasive tensions in her family is part of what makes her such a compelling character to us.

Growing Up, Growing Away

Baby boys, Dinah notices, are their mothers' pride and joy, doted on and adored. But when sons pass from infancy into childhood, they already start to cross over into the world of men, leaving the mother's side. Daughters, on the other hand, grow up in the mother's shadow. In this respect Dinah believes herself to be particularly blessed, the only daughter of Jacob's family. She knows each of her four mothers intimately, and her relationship with Leah, her own mother, is particularly important to her. "One of my great secrets was knowing I had the power to make her smile" (*Red Tent*, 83).

Yet Dinah soon realizes that Leah's life is more complicated than the mother-daughter bond they share. When Laban gambles away Ruti, and she appeals to Leah for help, Dinah can only watch as her mother presents Ruti's case to Jacob. "I saw the heat between my mother and her husband. I saw that Jacob could cause the glow of assent and happiness that I thought only I could summon from Leah" (*Red Tent*, 85). Dinah sees her father with new eyes and is impressed; yet she also understands a bit more of her parents' relationship with one another and finds herself excluded.

> There was no room for me between them, no need for me. My mother's eyes were full of Jacob. I did not matter to her the way she mattered to me. I wanted to cry, but I realized that I was too old for that. I would be a woman soon and I would have to learn how to live with a divided heart. (*Red Tent*, 86)

Eventually Dinah discovers that not only can she live with a divided heart, but she can keep it from the women who know her best. When she first meets Shalem, the awkwardness of their encounter is amplified by the sudden realization that she will not relate this event and her feelings to her mother. After she returns from her first trip to the town of Shechem, she is both delighted and dismayed to find that she is able to keep her newfound love a secret: "Before my trip to Shechem, I had supposed that my mothers could see my thoughts and look directly into my heart. But now I discovered that I was separate, opaque, and drawn into an orbit of which they had no knowledge" (*Red Tent*, 185).

Dinah comes of age physically in the company of her mothers, in the red tent, surrounded by their love. But she also comes of age emotionally and recognizes that she is a separate person, with private feelings and the ability to contemplate rebellion from her family's wishes and values. In this, Dinah is every bit the modern adolescent, whose coming of age is chronicled in countless novels from *The Catcher in the Rye* to *The Secret Life of Bees* and *Ellen Foster*.

Dinah's intimacy with Shalem separates her from her family of birth. In the midst of her joy with her new lover,

Dinah is pained by her father's and brothers' unwillingness to accept this match, but even more distressed by Leah's reaction. Recalling the episode later, Dinah envisions her mother as already distant.

> I wonder if she thought of me at all then, if she suffered over whether I had consented or cried out, if her heart reached out to discover whether I wept or rejoiced. But her words spoke only of the loss of a daughter, gone to the city where she would reside with foreign women, learn their ways, and forget her mother. (*Red Tent*, 195)

Dinah has not forgotten her mother. She regales Shalem with tales about her family, her mothers and her brothers, and gladly receives her aunt Bilhah when she comes for a brief visit. Yet in another sense she has already forgotten them, and they her. Never again will they relate to one another as they did before. Dinah will never again enter the red tent with her mothers and other women kinfolk. Indeed, she leaves the red tent behind completely, because she will live out her life among women who do not mark their monthly period with a time of seclusion together.

When Simon and Levi bring her home, her mothers bathe her and tend to her, but she stays only long enough to regain her strength and to call down curses on Jacob and her brothers. Then she leaves—not only the men, but her mothers too. "I walked away from love as well, never again to see my reflection in my mothers' eyes. But I could not live among them" (*Red Tent*, 207).

Husbands and Lovers

Although the focus of this novel is on women, the men who are most prominently featured are presented as gentle, caring, and loving in their sexual relationships. Even for all the vitriol that Dinah bears for her father, Jacob, she faithfully recounts her mothers' stories of their experiences with him, as he tries to make each of his four wives feel comfortable and welcome in his arms. Dinah describes Shalem in the laudatory terms of first, lost love; Benia is the patient, mature, caring lover.

Diamant's characters are no strangers to abusive relationships. Laban is presented as a brutish husband, physically and psychologically abusive to Ruti and an example to his sons, who disrespect her as well. But what is likely new to many of Diamant's readers is the notion that the relationships of biblical husbands and wives could be tender and loving. Her descriptions make these relationships, in all their variety, believable and enjoyable.

Jacob, Husband of Four Wives

While most of Dinah's portrait of her family is of the four sisters who share a husband, she also allows us glimpses of the man whom these four women share, both through retellings of her mothers' stories and her own observations. In Diamant's version Rachel is not in charge of the scheme to substitute Leah as Jacob's first wife, nor is she present, as the rabbis would have it, lurking under the bed and answering to hide Leah's voice. Jacob is apparently not deceived by the substitution of Leah for Rachel, nor does he object to it.

Rather, as Leah relates the story later, Jacob shows no surprise when he removes the bridal veil. Their week together is filled with laughter and lovemaking and companionship, sweeter for the realization that they will never have such a time together again. Jacob's rage at the substitution of Leah for Rachel, Dinah tells us, is feigned, a plot hatched between himself and Leah.

The week of marital harmony between Jacob and Leah does not escape Rachel's notice, and she is jealous of Leah and furious with Jacob. Dinah narrates Jacob's response:

> When her tears were spent, Jacob held her to his chest until it seemed she was asleep, and told her that she was the moon's own daughter, luminous, radiant, and perfect. That his love for her was worshipful. That he felt only duty toward Leah, who was a mere shadow of Rachel's light. That she, only Rachel, would be the bride of his heart, his first wife, first love. Such pretty treason. (*Red Tent*, 36)

When Bilhah, Rachel's handmaid, goes in to Jacob, she is a slave rather than a wife, and she has only a night with him, not a week. Yet he is a gentle and satisfying lover with her as well. Only Zilpah finds no pleasure with Jacob, although she acknowledges that this is her lack and not his. He is attentive and seeks to win her over, as he has her three sisters.

Jacob, in Dinah's retelling, is hardly a character of unalloyed goodness. He is capable of weakness and vacillation, and does not always handle well his role of leadership as head of household. His relationship with his daughter, Dinah, is nearly nonexistent. When he speaks with Hamor concerning her, he has trouble conjuring up a memory of her face. With his wives, too, Jacob seems sometimes to enter the game of playing them off, one against the other, for his own purposes. Yet Jacob's care for all four women is clear, and he neither abuses them nor refuses to listen to their concerns or their counsel. Except in the fateful case of Dinah's relationship with Shalem, in which Rachel and Zilpah encourage him to accept the match, Jacob seems to have as much respect for his wives as for his sons. His relationships with them show Jacob's complicated humanity.

Shalem

Like Jacob, most of the people whom Dinah describes in the pages of *The Red Tent* emerge as complex characters with both strengths and flaws. The exception is Dinah's lover Shalem, prince of Shechem. From their first meeting, the terms in which she describes him are glowing, almost reverent: "He was a firstborn son, the handsomest and quickest of the king's children, well liked by the people of Shechem. He was golden and beautiful as a sunset...He was perfect" (*Red Tent*, 183). Shalem compares favorably with Dinah's brothers, just as strong, but not so dirty as they. In his presence, Dinah is uncomfortable with her own appearance and does not know what to say or do.

Dinah soon learns that her interest in Shalem is requited, and through his mother's machinations they find themselves with the solitude necessary to consummate their relationship. Dinah recalls the pleasures of their lovemaking, the beauty of his body, the delights of their shared intimacy, the splendid food that they eat, and the scented water in which they bathe. Their days and nights pass as if in a dream, marked only slightly by the knowledge that Dinah's bride-price is being negotiated. The agreement that Shalem, like the rest of the men of Shechem, will be circumcised troubles Dinah; but Shalem promises that even this will be nothing more than a dream in their time to come.

The dream, of course, ends as a nightmare, more horrible for the fact that it is real. Shalem dies in Dinah's arms, and all their plans and dreams die with him. He remains in her memory the perfect lover, gone forever.

In a sense, Shalem remains a dream for Dinah. She has spent only a few days with him, and during those days the pair is provided with everything for their comfort and pleasure, not unlike Leah and Jacob during their week in the bridal tent. Dinah builds her memory of Shalem on these few experiences. Whether Dinah and Shalem would have become successful married lovers and parents, or whether there would eventually have been someone or something else between them, is a question forever left unanswered.

Benia

Dinah goes to Egypt with Re-nefer, bears her child there, and does not seek married love. After many years, when Re-mose has left for schooling and Dinah has become a midwife again, she encounters a carpenter named Benia, who speaks with gentleness and has strong, capable hands. She purchases a box from him and entertains the idea that there might be something between them: "[T]his was nothing like what I felt when I first saw Shalem. No hot wind blew through Benia and into me. This feeling was much cooler and calmer. Even so, my heart beat faster and I knew my eyes were brighter than they had been earlier in the day" (*Red Tent*, 247).

Two years later, after Re-nefer's death and in a different city in Egypt, Benia and Dinah meet once again. We learn that Meryt has located the carpenter and persuaded him to visit the house where Dinah is living. Reunited with Benia and finally able to accept his love, Dinah leaves with Meryt's blessing: "Go, in the name of the lady Isis and her consort Osiris. Go and be content" (*Red Tent*, 270). Dinah becomes a wife again, once more without a wedding, but this time for a long and happy marriage.

Benia not only is Dinah's husband and lover but also is her companion in ways that Jacob was never the companion of his wives. He and Dinah share stories, laugh together, delight in one another's accomplishments, and forgive one another's shortcomings, such as Dinah's inability to cook. He accompanies her to see Jacob's family when Jacob is on his deathbed. Although the trip is bittersweet for Dinah, she takes joy in Benia's delight at the finds in the marketplace.

Dinah's marriage to Benia lasts the rest of her life. When she dies, Benia cradles her face in his hands and weeps for her. He is the only man in her parting thoughts. She sees the faces of her mothers and the other women in her life, but besides them is only Benia, "a beacon as bright as the sun, and his light warmed me through and through" (*Red Tent*, 320). Even in death she does not leave him, so great is their love for each other.

Dinah and Benia's relationship is a strong argument that mature relationships need not be a mere shadow of younger loves. Each of them cherishes the memory of a first love now dead, and each respects the pain of the other's loss. Although they tell each other their stories, they leave some distance as well. Dinah recounts, "Neither of us ever gave voice to the names of our beloved dead ones, and for this act of respect they permitted us to live in peace with our new mates and never haunted our thoughts by day or visited our dreams at night" (*Red Tent*, 276).

Yet despite their separate histories and their lack of children together, Dinah and Benia find fulfillment in each other. One of the reasons *The Red Tent* is such a satisfying novel to read is that it ends with its main character, who has known such wrenching loss, having found true and enduring conjugal love as well.

Mother of Another Woman's Son

When Dinah leaves her home for the last time, after Simon and Levi have brought her back from Shechem, she has no thoughts of anything or anyone past herself and her dead lover. Yet the possibility that Dinah may be pregnant with

Shalem's child is enough to cause his mother, Re-nefer, to care more for Dinah's life than Dinah cares for it herself. She tends Dinah through the journey to Egypt. When it is clear that Dinah is, in fact, pregnant, Re-nefer spells out the terms on which both Dinah and the infant will be welcomed into Re-nefer's family.

It takes Dinah some time to adjust to all that this new status will mean. She is Shalem's widow, but as if she had been a slave wife, not freeborn. She is in the position of Zilpah or Bilhah, not Leah or Rachel. Her child, the fruit of her womb, will not be her own, and others will make the important decisions concerning his upbringing and education. Yet this status will be to her son's benefit, as he will be a member of a royal family. It is a bitter pill for Dinah to swallow, but she quickly understands that she has no choice.

So Dinah becomes a mother, assisting in her own labor by instructing the Egyptian midwife, Meryt, how to cut her and turn the baby so that he can be safely delivered. She holds her son for the first time and knows that she has passed over from childhood. "I beheld myself as an infant in my mother's arms, and caught a glimpse of my own death. I wept without knowing whether I rejoiced or mourned. My mothers and their mothers were with me as I held my baby" (*Red Tent*, 226).

Yet the next time Dinah awakens, she is told that her son, Re-mose, is "with his mother" and learns the difficult truth of bearing a child on another woman's knees. She will be his nurse, and he will always know that she gave him birth, but she is not his mother, not in Egypt. He will stay with her until he is ready for school, but she realizes that more than this she is not promised. She whispers "Bar-Shalem" into his tiny ear, but Re-nefer rebukes her sharply:

> Without turning to look at me she said, "If you call him by that name again, I will have you thrown out of this house and into the street. If you do not heed my instructions in this, and in all matters regarding the education of our son, you will lose him. You must understand this completely." (*Red Tent*, 227–28)

Dinah complies with Re-nefer's commands. She has no other choice, for although she knows no one in Egypt outside Re-nefer's family, Egypt is her only home.

Re-mose grows into a toddler and then a boy and begins sleeping on the roof of the house instead of in the garden with Dinah. At nine, he is sent to school in Memphis to become a scribe like his uncle, and Dinah finds herself lonelier than ever before. Over the next few years, Dinah sees her son only rarely, and each time she feels more keenly the distance between them. He speaks fondly and politely to her, but they do not share their sorrows, nor do they speak of the future. Still, Dinah holds out hope that her son will one day make room for his mother in his life.

Then comes the fateful incident in the house of the vizier Zafenat Paneh-ah, when Dinah realizes that her son's master is her brother Joseph. The stage is set for a confrontation between Dinah's son and a brother of the men who killed his father. Such a meeting cannot bode well for Dinah, who will not be able to hold onto them both. Re-mose unleashes on Joseph all the pent-up anger of a lifetime of living as an orphan, and he vows revenge on his master. Joseph recognizes the danger in Re-mose's challenge and uses his power to have him placed under guard. Dinah intervenes, but Joseph insists that her son must be sent away or else executed for his threats. Dinah is powerless to change Joseph's mind, or the course of events.

When Dinah sees Re-mose again, it is to say a final farewell. He does not acknowledge her presence, so she makes her speech to his back. She tells him good-bye and asks his forgiveness for keeping from him the secret of his birth. She speaks Shalem's name to her son for the first time, and she leaves him with a benediction.

> "I will remember you in the morning and in the evening, every day until I close my eyes forever. I forgive your every harsh thought of me and the curses you may hurl at my name. And when at last you do forgive me, I forbid you to suffer a moment's guilt in my name. I ask that you remember only my blessing upon you, Bar-Shalem Re-mose."

My son did not move from his couch or say a word, and I took my leave, brokenhearted but free. (*Red Tent*, 295)

As all parents know, children grow up and move away. Whether they are physically absent or not, grown children cannot stay in the place in their mothers' hearts that they occupied when they were small. Dinah's experience with Re-mose exemplifies this truism in starkest terms. She begins to be separated from her son even before he is born, when his father dies and she leaves her home and family behind. His place in Egyptian society is predicated on secrets and half-truths, one consequence of which is the loss of her legal status as his freeborn mother. She relinquishes all ties to him to protect his life and his future. Most mothers, fortunately, do not face such an extreme choice. Still, many a mother knows the pain of loving a child enough to let him or her go, recognizing that although she may have been the very center of this beloved child's past, she will have no significant part in his or her future.

New Mothers, New Daughters

After Dinah leaves her home, she never sees her mothers again. She never bears children besides Re-mose. Yet the years she spends in Egypt after Re-mose is gone from her are in many ways the richest of her life. She gradually learns to love again and gathers around herself a new, surrogate family.

The first person to whom Dinah grows close is Meryt, the midwife who attended Re-mose's birth. The two women are bound by the midwife's profession, although at first Dinah refuses to leave her house to accompany Meryt to births. Gradually, Dinah begins to see in Meryt what she loved in her own mothers. Meryt's skin is the color of Bilhah's. Her passion for bringing babies safely into the world rivals Rachel's. Meryt's sons are grown, her husband is dead, and she comes to treat the younger woman as her own daughter.

After Dinah's reunion with Benia, she no longer lives with Meryt's family, but Meryt visits often, frequently with grand-children in tow. One of these, Kiya, becomes a familiar presence in Dinah and Benia's house and relates to Dinah as daughter to mother.

Dinah is present at Meryt's deathbed. The older midwife's final gift to her is to make Dinah one of her family. Dinah takes the role of oldest female relative, preparing Meryt's body for burial. After Meryt's death, Dinah meets her own mothers once again in her dreams.

Finally Dinah takes her place, in her turn, as the matriarch:

> With Meryt gone, I was the wise woman, the mother, the grandmother, and even great-grandmother of those around me. Shif-re, a new grandmother, and Kiya, about to be married, attended me wherever I went to place the bricks. They learned what I had to teach, and soon went on their own to deliver women from the fear and loneliness of birth. My apprentices became sister and daughter. In them, I found new water in the well I thought would remain forever dry after my Meryt died. (*Red Tent*, 302)

Dinah becomes grandmother to Kiya's children, who light her last days. Kiya is present as Dinah's daughter when she dies. Thus the end of Dinah's life, like the beginning, is full of women and children.

Brother Dearest

For readers familiar with the Bible, perhaps no character portrayed in Diamant's novel is as intriguing as her portrait of Joseph, son of Rachel. In Genesis, Joseph is first a victim, then a hero. His arrogance is excused by his unusual experience: when he tells his brothers his visions of their obeisance to him, is he not simply speaking the truth about his dreams? His brothers, surely, are completely in the wrong for seeking to be done with him and then deceiving their father about the fate of the beloved firstborn child of his Rachel. Joseph's rise from slavery and obscurity in Egypt is clearly the result of his wisdom and of divine favor. Although his behavior with his brothers seems petty, the reader of Genesis is encouraged to concur with Joseph's own evaluation of the whole situation: "God intended it for good" (Gen. 50:20).

Diamant's Dinah, naturally, tells us a great deal about Joseph as a young child: "As a baby, Joseph was my constant companion, first my milk-brother and later my truest friend" (*Red Tent*, 75). When Dinah and Joseph are together, they tell each other the stories they have heard, Joseph of the gods of their forefathers, Dinah the tales that her mothers have related to her.

Dinah and Joseph share a powerful experience when they happen upon the place where their father wrestled with the angel. They escape from a charging boar, but the experience leaves an imprint on them both, especially on Joseph. Dinah says: "My brother was never the same. From that night forward, he began to dream with the power of our father's dreams. At first, he spoke of his wondrous encounters with angels and demons, with dancing stars and talking beasts, to me only. Soon, his dreams were too big for my ears alone" (*Red Tent*, 125).

Despite all they share as children, though, Dinah takes leave of Joseph as completely as the rest of his brothers. She has no knowledge of his later exploits until she finally realizes who he is, in Joseph's own house in Thebes after she has delivered his son. By this time, both Re-mose and Shery have described the man they know as Zafenat Paneh-ah. Re-mose's account of the vizier is colored by his ambition, because he sees his own fortunes as being constricted by Zafenat Paneh-ah's service. He does not respect his master's vaunted skill in interpreting dreams and feels keenly the restriction of serving as scribe to this illiterate foreigner, who is completely dependent on him and whose good fortune has come at the expense of his own.

Shery, a servant in Zafenat Paneh-ah's household, mocks her master's story of a rise from lowly beginnings and implies that his rise from slavery had primarily to do with his good looks and how he used them. She, too, scoffs at his dream-interpreting abilities, attributing them to the gullibility of those who saw him as an oracle. Still, Shery admires Zafenat Paneh-ah's ability to accumulate power, and she recounts his story in detail, so that both the reader and Dinah finally recognize in the tale Joseph, son of Jacob.

Dinah's presence in his house shocks and unnerves Joseph. He treats her kindly, but there is no reconciliation between them. Yet when Jacob is dying and sends for Joseph so that his sons may receive their grandfather's blessing, Joseph comes to get Dinah and take her with him. Although they travel together, Joseph and Dinah grow no closer. She can no longer find the brother she once knew in this powerful, self-absorbed man. When they take their leave of each other, they part tenderly, but without grief.

Relationships between siblings are shaped by a number of factors: gender, birth order, difference in ages, the number of children in the family. Sometimes siblings grow up sharing a living space and parents, but little else. At other times, though, a special relationship grows between siblings, so that they become an integral part of each other's experience of growing up. These relationships may continue into adulthood, and siblings are sometimes the truest of adult friends. Or, as is the case with Dinah and Joseph, siblings who were close as children may become adults who can no longer find the companion they once knew. They may see each other, perhaps uncharitably, through the eyes of strangers. Children's fraternal love can be powerful, but it is also fragile. When siblings reach adulthood, their childhood love for brothers and sisters sometimes dies.

A Stranger to Her Kin, a Legend in Her Time

The trip to Jacob's deathbed affords Dinah one opportunity she relishes: the chance to see the grandchildren of her mothers. She believes herself to be no longer interested in her brothers. As she has already told Joseph, they "are no more to me than the livestock of our youth" (*Red Tent*, 294). Yet once she sees them, she is grieved that they do not know her, and she begins to recall their childhood days.

I remembered Reuben's kindness and Judah's beauty. I remembered Dan's voice in song and the way Gad and Asher mimicked our grandfather until I collapsed in laughter. I remembered how Issa and Tali wept when Levi and Simon tormented them and said they were interchangeable in their mother's eyes. I remembered how Judah once tickled me until I peed, but never told a soul. I remembered how Reuben used to carry me on his shoulders, from where I could touch the clouds. (*Red Tent*, 311)

Joseph reports that Jacob does not remember his daughter or express remorse for what happened to her. "He said nothing of you. Dinah is forgotten in the house of Jacob" (*Red Tent*, 312).

However, Dinah learns that her brother's assessment is incorrect. While none of her young relatives recognize her, she is still part of the family's lore. Gera, Benjamin's daughter, tells the tale she has heard from her Aunt Ahavah to the woman she assumes is a nurse to Joseph's sons. Leah's sole surviving daughter, Gera says, was a great beauty, taken in marriage by the son of King Hamor. The king himself offered the bride-price and doubled it when Simon and Levi made noisy objections, claiming that their sister had been kidnapped and raped. Still suspicious, they tried to undo the marriage by insisting on the circumcision of the Shechemites as part of the bride-price. Gera continues:

"Now comes the part of this story that makes me think it is nothing more than a tale that girls tell each other. The prince submitted to the knife! He and his father and all the men in the city! My cousins say this is impossible, because men are not capable of such love." (*Red Tent*, 316)

In somber tones she relates the rest of the story, the slaughter wrought by Levi and Simon, the plunder of the city, Simon's Shechemite wife and their son, who committed suicide when he learned the story of his father's villainy.

My eyes had been fixed upon my spindle as she recounted the tale. "And what of the sister?" I asked. "The one who was loved by the prince?"

"That is a mystery," said Gera. "I think she died of grief. Serah made up a song about her being gathered by the Queen of Heaven and turned into a falling star."

"Is her name remembered?" I asked softly.
"Dinah," she said. "I like the sound of it, don't
you? Someday, if I am delivered of a daughter, I will
call her Dinah." (*Red Tent*, 317)

Dinah leaves Jacob's sons' home in peace, secure in the
knowledge that her story is too terrible to be forgotten. She
also leaves with Rachel's lapis ring, a gift from Judah, the
only member of her father's family who acknowledges
knowing who she is. Leah, he says, told him to give it to her
daughter, although he had long assumed he would never
see Dinah again.

Wondering later why Leah would send her Rachel's ring,
Dinah hopes she will find the answer in a dream. Benia,
though, is her oracle. "Perhaps your mother meant it as a
token that she had forgiven her sister. Maybe it was a sign
that she died with an undivided heart, and wished the same
for you" (*Red Tent*, 318).

Although she is no longer known to the children and
grandchildren of those who gave her birth, Dinah does, it
seems, end her life with an undivided heart. She has loved
deeply, grieved unreservedly, and found family when there
was none. She has been able to say good-bye and to be freed
of the past. And she knows that in the generations to come,
she will be remembered, both by those she has come to love
and among her own kin. As Dinah herself says, "It is more
than enough."

QUESTIONS FOR DISCUSSION

---

1. Dinah is nearly as close to her aunts as to her own mother.
   Did you experience a particularly close relationship with
   a member of your extended family of origin? What gifts,
   as Dinah speaks of her relationship with her aunts, did
   that person give to you?

2. What skills did you learn from your mother, or from
   someone who was like a mother to you? How have they
   shaped the person you are today? Are there areas in

which your mother excelled that you never mastered? In what areas have you exceeded your mother's skill?

3. What tensions characterized your family of origin? What did you learn from negotiating these difficulties?

4. Were you surprised at the depth of love and affection that Dinah narrates between biblical husbands and wives? Does this perspective give you a new way to think about the stories of biblical couples?

5. What events most clearly marked your process of separation from your parents, or, if you have grown children, their separation from you? Are they memories of joy or pain?

For Further Reading

Essex, Barbara J. *Krazy Kinfolk: Exploring Dysfunctional Families of the Bible.* Cleveland: Pilgrim Press, 2005.

Gilbert, Roberta M. *Connecting With Our Children: Guiding Principles for Parents in a Troubled World.* New York: John Wiley & Sons, 1999.

Jordan, Merle R. *Reclaiming Your Story: Family History and Spiritual Growth.* Louisville: Westminster John Knox Press, 1999.

Miller-McLemore, Bonnie J. *Also a Mother: Work and Family as Theological Dilemma.* Nashville: Abingdon Press, 1994.

Moessner, Jeanne Stevenson, ed. *In Her Own Time: Women and Developmental Issues in Pastoral Care.* Minneapolis: Fortress Press, 2000.

CHAPTER 6

Retelling the Story

*Hidden in all stories is the One story. The more we
listen, the clearer that Story becomes. Our true identity, who
we are, why we are here, what sustains us, is in this story.
The stories at every kitchen table are about the same things,
stories of owning, of having and losing, of sex, of power, of
pain, of wounding, of courage, hope, and healing, of
loneliness and the end of loneliness. Stories about God.*

(*Kitchen Table Wisdom,*[1] xxix)

Give ear, O my people, to my teaching;
    incline your ears to the words of my mouth.
I will open my mouth in a parable;
    I will utter dark sayings from of old,
things that we have heard and known,
    that our ancestors have told us.

(Ps. 78:1–3)

Not only is *The Red Tent* a finely crafted story, it is a story
about telling a story. The entire novel is presented to us as
the first-person narrative of its main character. So compelling

[1]Rachel Naomi Remen, *Kitchen Table Wisdom: Stories That Heal* (New York:
Riverhead Books, 1996).

is this storytelling persona that we are not upset when our narrator reveals that she is speaking to us from beyond the grave. Indeed, by the end of the book we have come to think of death as so much an integral part of life that we would likely feel cheated if Dinah did *not* narrate her own death and the continuing life of her loved ones afterward.

In presenting her story to us, Dinah is eloquent and straightforward. Although she exists only in our imagination, there she is a very strong presence. We imagine her speaking to us in a clear and steady tone, telling us even the painful details without flinching.

Telling Our Stories: Releasing the Pain

As Dinah the narrator reminds us, she was not always so forthcoming. We hear from the opening pages of the novel that personal and family stories are important, and we observe young Dinah learning her mothers' stories. We may not realize until much later how reticent Dinah has been about her own story, and how painful her silence has been to her. Dinah finally tells her whole story for the first time to Werenro, sometime servant to Dinah's grandmother Rebecca, after she discovers that the veiled singer who has come to her home in Egypt is her old acquaintance.

> Without hesitation, I told her everything. I leaned my head back, closed my eyes, and gave voice to my life. In all of my years, I had never before spoken so much or so long, and yet the words came effortlessly, as though this were something I had done many times before.
>
> I surprised myself, remembering Tabea, remembering Ruti, remembering my coming of age in the red tent. I spoke of Shalem and our passionate love-making without blushing. I spoke of our betrayal and his murder. I told her about Re-nefer's bargain with me, and Meryt's care for me, and I spoke of my son with pride and love.
>
> It was not difficult. Indeed, it was as though I had been parched and there was cool water in my mouth.

I said "Shalem" and my breath was clean after years of being foul and bitter. I called my son "Bar-Shalem," and an old tightness in my chest eased.

I recited the names of my mothers, and knew with total certainty that they were dead. I leaned my face into Werenro's shoulder and soaked her robe in memory of Leah and Rachel, Zilpah and Bilhah. (*Red Tent*, 255–56)

When Dinah has finished, Werenro, who has also recounted her bitter experience, recognizes that that Dinah's "grief shines from your heart." But, Werenro says Dinah's grief serves a positive purpose. "The flame of love is strong," she says. "Your story is not finished, Dinah."

Dinah is a storyteller from early in life, and she grows up in the midst of storytellers. Her mothers, especially her aunts Zilpah and Bilhah, relate the stories of gods and goddesses. Dinah and Joseph swap the stories they have each heard from their elders, and for a time they keep a few of their brothers as playmates by regaling them with stories. When Dinah meets her cousin Tabea, Esau's daughter, they tell one another the stories of their families. Even in the arms of her young lover, Dinah is a storyteller, recounting the tales of her family to Shalem until she imagines that he knows many of them better than Jacob himself.

Yet Dinah is prevented from telling the story that matters most to her. Soon after their arrival in Egypt, Re-nefer spells out the terms by which Dinah will live in her family's house and by which Dinah's child will be given a new identity. It is a spare story, glossing over many of the most important details, but Re-nefer insists on this telling. Dinah knows that such a recounting will never release her from her pain.

We never wept or mourned over Shalem, nor did she tell where my beloved was buried. The horror was to remain unspoken, my grief sealed behind my lips. We never again spoke of our shared history, and I was bound to the emptiness of the story she told. (*Red Tent*, 215)

Therapists and counselors know that events that remain unspoken retain their power to hurt and may even kill. When a patient is finally able to give voice to experience, no matter how terrible, she or he has taken the first step toward healing. Dinah's world is constricted to the present by the birth of her son, and for the first years of his life she lives willingly in that narrow world, shut off from past and future. Although she delights in Re-mose, it is a time of no growth for her, a time of no healing. Her story remains untold largely for his sake, and her silence serves to protect him. Her self-revelation to Werenro comes, significantly, at the feast celebrated to mark Re-mose's entrance into manhood, and thus his independence from his mother. Dinah is freed to take the first step, however cautiously, toward her own freedom.

Telling Our Stories: Establishing Community

The second time that Dinah recounts her story, she has much more to tell. By this time she is the wife of Benia the carpenter. In her service as midwife she has encountered her brother Joseph, now the king's vizier, and has said good-bye to her son. All this, as well as the story of her childhood and the events that brought her to Egypt, she narrates to her good friend and fellow midwife Meryt:

> After I was at peace and still, I asked her to sit by my side and I took her hand, still warm and moist with oil, and told her the rest of what had happened to me in Thebes, including how it came to pass that Zafenat Paneh-ah, the king's right hand, was my brother Joseph.
>
> Meryt listened in stillness, watching my face as I recounted my mothers' history, and the story of Shechem and the murder of Shalem. My friend did not move or utter a sound, but her face revealed the workings of her heart, showing me horror, rage, sympathy, compassion.
>
> When I finished, she shook her head. "I see why you did not tell me this before," she said sadly. "I wish I had been able to help you bear this burden

from the very first. But now that you entrust your past to my keeping, it is safe. I know you need no oath from me, or else you would not have told me.

"Dear one," she said, putting her hand to my cheek, "I am so honored to be the vessel into which you pour this story of pain and strength. For all these years, no daughter could have made me happier or more proud than you. Now that I know who you are and what life has cost you, I am in awe that I number you among my beloved." (*Red Tent*, 298)

Meryt already considers Dinah her daughter. But when Dinah tells Meryt her whole story, a new and stronger bond is forged between them. Dinah's story is no less dangerous than it was before. It could still be used to hurt her further. In the wrong hands it could still threaten the well-being of her son, Re-mose. Yet Dinah is not afraid to speak her story to Meryt. She feels at ease, once again capable of trust, so that she is able to recount the story of her deepest betrayal. When she is done, both Dinah and Meryt are changed, and the relationship between them is altered. Stories have the power to form connections between human beings, to establish community where none existed before.

Besides Dinah, several other people tell their stories in this novel. In part, this is a literary device Diamant employs to help her readers keep straight a large cast of characters. But beyond being an author's trick, the personal stories told by the various characters show the relationships they form with one another.

Werenro, as the veiled Egyptian sistrum-player, sings her epic tale of love found and lost as a performance, albeit a compelling, almost magical one. It is not Werenro's own story, and it does not bring the singer closer to her listeners. Indeed, it serves to distance her from them even further, making her seem an unearthly apparition. Werenro tells her personal story to Dinah, but unlike Dinah, Werenro does not allow herself to experience her own tale's emotion: "There is nothing in my heart. I care for no one, and for nothing. ... It is not so bad to be dead" (*Red Tent*, 255). Nonetheless, Werenro holds Dinah while the younger woman tells her story for the first time, and Dinah imagines that Werenro's voice holds "a little sorrow" when she proclaims Dinah, unlike herself, alive. For a few moments they experience the peace of shared pain; but when Dinah awakens, Werenro is gone.

Benia tells Dinah his story expecting—and for some time receiving—nothing in return. His personal narrative, even the painful details, is ongoing evidence to Dinah that he can be trusted, that he will remain faithful and loving. He is the only man whose story we hear in detail in the book. His retelling of his story ultimately makes it possible for Dinah to tell him hers.

Meryt invents a story of Dinah's past that eases her entry into her new community in Egypt. Shery's story of Zafenat Paneh-ah furthers the plot, summarizing details we know from a different perspective from the stories of Genesis. And Gera's family narrative comes full circle, returning to Dinah's own role as keeper of her mothers' stories and assuring Dinah that her tale, and her name, will not be forgotten among her people. All of these show us the web of relationships that narrative forms, a web that supports and sustains us.

In addition *The Red Tent* offers us the gift of making us good listeners. These days we rarely listen intently to the long personal story of another. Our listening skills are poorly developed, and we do not give much thought to practicing them. We have learned somewhere along the way that being a good conversationalist means having something to contribute to the discussion. So when someone relates a personal story, as often as not we respond with the account of a similar personal experience, or the experience of someone we know, deflecting attention from the first narrative, and quite likely keeping the rest of that particular story from being told. Few of us are trained or intentional listeners, aware of the invitation present in attentive silence.

Dinah greets us, her readers, welcomes us and acknowledges that we want to hear her story, and then pours out the tale. She assumes that we want to listen. She does not pause to see if we have found a way to relate. Perhaps at points we do. At other times the story is remarkably strange to us, yet we continue to listen. We are forced to be mute listeners, and we find that we enjoy, even crave, this unaccustomed role.

We may or may not be the perfect audience. Some readers consume the whole novel at one sitting, oblivious to interruptions. Others read casually, a bit at a time. Some skip through chapters, flipping to the end, scanning pages until something catches the eye. But our narrator knows none of that. Having welcomed us as guests, she continues to treat us as guests, serving up her best storytelling for our consumption. When it is complete, she thanks us for our kindness in accompanying her through the story and speaks a word of blessing to us.

Thus we, as readers, begin to think of ourselves as Dinah, our narrator, sees us. We think of ourselves as good listeners—whether we are or not—and begin to recognize the value of the art of listening. And as we reflect on the experience of hearing Dinah's story, we may start to pay attention to other stories we hear around us. If Dinah's story has done its work, we will listen to those other stories more attentively, without trying immediately to relate them to our own. We will uncover the lost art of listening, just listening, and know that, like Dinah, those whose stories we hear will bless us simply for the gift of our presence.

Telling Our Stories: Becoming Whole

Several years later, Dinah tells her story one more time. Joseph's second son has been born. Although Dinah's services as midwife are not needed, Joseph sends a generous payment anyway. Such strange behavior arouses her husband's curiosity, and she is finally ready to explain.

> When Benia asked me why the gift was so extravagant, I told him everything.
>
> It was the third time I had given voice to the full story; first to Werenro, then to Meryt. But this time my heart did not pound nor my eyes fill as I told it. It was only a story from the distant past. (*Red Tent*, 299)

Dinah experiences her own life as a story. She is not distanced from her subject; on the contrary, she is deeply and vitally involved with the events and people she narrates. But neither is she judgmental. She reports on both the good and the bad sides of her characters, and allows us to see them as whole, complex persons. We understand both Leah's pain and Rachel's, and the animosity between them, but Dinah does not compel us to take sides. We understand Dinah's undying gratitude toward Re-nefer as well as her deep pain at her mother-in-law's unwillingness to speak Shalem's name or to allow Dinah to call her son after his father.

Nor does Dinah judge herself. She does not lord her successes over others or wallow in her mistakes. She feels deeply, hurts deeply, loves deeply, but ultimately is able to take what life hands her. She does not pretend, as Re-nefer does, that she can get on with life by putting difficult events behind her. Instead she lives her entire life, the good and the bad. She retells the events until she is able to gain new understanding from them, and then continues to retell them, because they continue to yield new meanings, new wisdom.

We discover that Dinah has been able to grow from her experiences by realizing that it could have been otherwise. Just after she narrates the slaughter of the Shechemites and the death of Shalem, Dinah tells us what would have happened to her had her family succeeded in bringing and keeping her home. She would have been present to witness the rest of the lives of her family members. She would have seen her brothers' betrayal of Joseph and Jacob's estrangement from Reuben. She would have witnessed the decline of her mothers, and, she vows, she would have treated Rachel and Leah with greater kindness than they experienced in their deaths.

But Dinah also foresees that she would have lost her baby. She would have lived out her days in anger and bitterness, "a blot upon the earth." "I might have walked and wept for many years more, half mad, finishing my days in the doorway of a lesser brother's third wife. But my life would have been finished" (*Red Tent*, 208).

"But the gods had other plans for me," Dinah says (*Red Tent*, 210). Re-nefer and her steward Nehesi take her with them to Egypt. Her son does not die, but lives. When the truth of his past catches up to him and threatens his life again,

Dinah once more chooses life for him, by letting him go from her forever. Werenro is right: in Dinah there is a strong will to live. She lives not in spite of her experiences but through them, and ultimately because of them. We continue to read her story because of the person her life has shaped her to be. Dinah loves herself as she is and loves her life as it is, and we, her readers, love her for it.

Because Dinah embraces all of life, she does not fear death. She attributes this attitude in part to her training as a midwife. Startled to learn that her cousin and new friend Tabea does not want children, she says that she is not afraid of the pain of childbirth or the risk of death to herself or the infant. She discovers that she thinks of herself as a midwife, Rachel's apprentice and Inna's granddaughter. She is the only one among the women who is able to look on Leah's stillborn daughter: "I was not afraid to hold that small death" (*Red Tent*, 141). Later, as a practicing midwife, all her training has given her tools to outwit the death-god Anubis, but she also knows how to help a dying woman pass peacefully to the other side.

When Dinah's time comes to die, she knows only a little pain, and no fear. She is surrounded by those who love her. Benia cradles her face in his hands. She sees her mothers and all the other women who have nurtured her waiting to welcome her, and she goes willingly to join them.

> I felt nothing but excitement at the lessons that death held out to me. In the moment before I crossed over, I knew that the priests and magicians of Egypt were fools and charlatans for promising to prolong the beauties of life beyond the world we are given. Death is no enemy, but the foundation of gratitude, sympathy, and art. Of all life's pleasures, only love owes no debt to death. (*Red Tent*, 320)

Garrison Keillor, well-known storyteller and host of *A Prairie Home Companion*, is fond of saying regarding the denizens of his fictional Lake Wobegon, "It just becomes a story." The searing pain of the most humiliating experience fades, and it just becomes a story. A grievous wrong is recounted, but the point is no longer determining who is to blame; it has become a story. A woman lies dying, an iconoclast all her life who worried her friends and embarrassed her children, but they no longer have any reason to fret or to be ashamed; it all becomes a story. Dinah is comforted after Jacob's death to know that she has become a story. No one among her relatives may know her face when she appears among them, but she has already achieved immortality. She has become a story.

And the tale of Dinah is, of course, first and foremost a story. It is a story older and greater yet than the novel in which we have encountered it, truer than any particular historical claims we might be able to make about it. It is a story that arrests our attention, that bids us to listen, to consider, to ask new questions. It is a story that invites us to imagine other biblical stories as deeper and richer than the sparse manner in which they are narrated. And it is a story that invites us to bring ourselves into its narrative flow and to receive from it a blessing.

QUESTIONS FOR DISCUSSION

1. What stories do you know from your family of origin? How do you think you have been shaped by knowing— or not knowing—your family stories?

2. What stories do you tell when you are first establishing a friendship? Are there stories that you relate only to your most intimate friends?

3. Have you had the experience of keeping a story untold for a long while, then finally being able to tell it? What happened to make it possible for you to tell your story? What changed after you gave voice to it?

4. Consider the community of people among whom you feel most comfortable. How are relationships in that community built on shared stories?

5. Are you a good listener? What practices might you cultivate to help you become a better listener?

6. How have the personal stories of other people enriched your life? How might you relate your own story so that it is a blessing to others?

For Further Reading

Buechner, Frederick. *Telling Secrets*. New York: HarperSanFrancisco, 1991.

Healing Story Alliance Web site, www.healingstory.org.

Morgan, Richard L. *Remembering Your Story: Creating Your Own Spiritual Autobiography*. Nashville: Upper Room Books, 2002.

Remen, Rachel Naomi, M.D. *Kitchen Table Wisdom: Stories That Heal*. New York: Riverhead Books, 1996.